The Greatest Marvel of Nature

THE GREATEST MARVEL
OF NATURE

AN INTRODUCTION TO THE
PHILOSOPHY OF THE HUMAN PERSON

PIERRE-MARIE EMONET, O.P.

Translated by
Robert R. Barr

A Herder & Herder Book
The Crossroad Publishing Company
New York

The Crossroad Publishing Company
370 Lexington Avenue, New York, NY 10017

Original edition: *L'âme humaine expliqueé aux simples*
© 1994 by Éditions C.L.D., Chambray-lès-Tours, France

English translation © 2000 by The Crossroad Publishing Company

Printed in the United States of America

Library of Congress Cataloging-in-Publication Data

Emonet, Pierre-Marie.
    [Ame humaine expliquee aux simples. English]
    The greatest marvel of nature : an introduction to the philosophy of the human person / Pierre-Marie Emonet ; translated by Robert R. Barr.
       p. cm.
    ISBN 0-8245-1799-7
    1. Soul.   2. Philosophical anthropology.   I. Title.

BD422.F7 E4613 2000
128—dc21
                                   99-053599

1   2   3   4   5   6   7   8   9   10   04   03   02   01   00

Contents

v

Part 2
Human Beings: Their Intellectual Life

Part 3
Human Beings: Their Affective Life

Part 4
Human Beings: Their Freedom and Subjectivity

Contents   vii

Foreword

However far you may plumb the soul,
you will not find its floor,
so profound is the Word that dwells therein.

—Heraclitus, *Fragment* 45

THIS PRONOUNCEMENT, uttered by a Greek philosopher who lived in Ephesus in the sixth century before Christ, could well have discouraged us from writing on the human soul. But just the contrary occurred. To know that, in meditating on this subject, we were to plumb the depths of the human being, actually attracted us. For that matter, two centuries after Heraclitus, neither did another Greek philosopher shrink from undertaking this quest. We mean Aristotle. In his treatise *On the Soul*, Aristotle explained why the human soul has no boundaries: Because its nature opens out upon the infinite.

And so we undertake to set forth Aristotle's analyses. We address everyone. Our view is that everyone, and not just the expert in philosophy, has the right to be guided to the depths of the human person.

By way of a motto for our long reflection on the human soul, we offer the chant of the chorus in Sophocles' *Antigone:* "Many are the marvels of nature, but the greatest marvel of all is the human being" (333).

Part 1

The Human Being's Sensory Life

O *precious universe, in my knowing hands!*
—Paul Claudel

1

How Can One Discover the Existence of the Soul?

A fine way to know the soul is to regard the body.

—Paul Claudel

THE LATIN WORD FOR "SOUL," *anima,* comes from the Greek word for "wind," or "breath": *anemos.* By analogy with a breeze or gust of wind, we can already say something about the soul. The wind set things in motion. The tree filled with a gust of wind moves its branches. At that moment, we can say that the tree is "animated." And so we shall give the name "soul" to the foundation that communicates to certain natural bodies the faculty of moving themselves. This is the case with all living bodies: vegetation, animals, and human beings. Thus, we grasp the presence of the soul in a body by the movements that it spontaneously accomplishes from within. Claudel is right: A good way to know the soul is to begin by looking carefully at a living body.

A living body is a body that begins as a seed, an egg, a first cell, and thrusts spontaneously to the light. And it does so by providing itself, for example, like the plant, with roots, a stem, branches, leaves, blossoms. And all of these organs, these tools of future operations, are joined by the living being in a closely knit unit.

3

If we observe a living being in the course of formation, we notice that it possesses an inner foundation that guides its construction. This inner foundation, this living "principle," is the cause of operations so diversified that it takes three entirely different words to designate all of its virtualities. As that which sets in motion the material of its construction, it is rightly called *anima*, "soul." Inasmuch as this construction includes finely wrought and arranged organs, it is called "idea." And inasmuch as it makes of these many tools a perfectly structured whole, it is called "form." In his *On the Soul*, Aristotle uses these three words constantly. As we see, these three terms designate a single reality, but a reality too rich for one word to express all of its functions.

As we notice, it is impossible to speak of the soul without speaking of the body. Indeed, it is for itself, as it were, that the soul constructs the body. Aristotle is only describing what occurs in nature at every moment when he writes, "We see that the body exists for the purpose of the soul" (*The Parts of Animals* 645b.19). Again, he writes, "The first act of the soul is to organize the body for the purpose of a specific operation that it [the soul] has to accomplish" (ibid., 645b.16–18). Each organ exists for an altogether determinate activity. The soul creates the eye because it, the soul, is meant to see. The living body presents, as a unit, finely connected organs, for the purpose of a complex activity. Speaking of the rose in its first beginnings, the poet observes:

> [The rose] in the dead of winter and the uncertain spring,
>   gathers itself.
> Perfect among its thorny leaves, at last the red flower
> of desire, in its ardent geometry![1]

Yes, one need only observe a living body at the moment of its formation, and one contemplates its soul. Whether this observation, this contemplation, be performed after the fashion of the scientist, or the painter, or the poet, it is its soul that she will discover putting together the body it needs. The soul has need of the body in order, one day, to tell its secret, like "the rose that opens its pages to the breeze and can be read with closed eyes."

2

To What End Does the Human Soul Compose the Body It Has?

Blossoming of my being in the flower of all that is.
—Jacques Maritain

IF THE ROSE COMPOSES, gathers together, the body that belongs to it, it is in order at last to come to blossom and spread abroad its perfume. The bird composes its body for flight and song. Why does the human soul give its body this architecture? Or we can ask: What attracts the human zygote at the moment of its genesis? What specific operations does that cell prepare in fashioning the organs of the outer senses and, in the brain, the tools of the inner senses? All of these instruments, so delicately arranged!

One of the answers will be: If the human soul gives itself the body it has, it is not only in order to be born to itself; it is to be born to all that is, by the reception into it of all things. At the same time, the soul gives itself its body in order to let it, the soul, emerge from itself toward things, giving them its love. Knowledge and love—this is why the human soul gives itself its organs and keeps them together; this is the soul's ultimate raison d'être.

6

Let us begin at once to speak of the first "finality," or goal, purpose, of the human soul: knowledge.

The human soul grows organs for the purpose of being born twice. A line from Aristotle celebrates precisely the infinite breadth of the human soul: "The soul, in knowing, is in a certain way all things" (*On the Soul* 3.8.431b.21–22). What Heraclitus said—that we shall never sound the soul to its very floor—Aristotle explains thus: By knowledge, the human soul is capable of containing within itself all that is.

Having this intuition supposes that one realizes the evident: The sensory organs that constitute its body are ordained by the soul for knowledge. Is there any need to demonstrate this? The eye, the ear, the nose, the mouth are so many tools capable of grasping the qualities of things in order to absorb them. After all, it is not for biological ends alone that these organs and their faculties are exercised. It is not only in order to eat and destroy things that we are interested in things. Also, indeed often, it is simply in order to regard them, to contemplate them—for the pleasure of knowing them. Aristotle begins the *Metaphysics:* "All human beings, by nature, have the desire to know" (1.980a.21).

Let us attempt to state the mystery of knowledge. We shall transcribe here certain lines written by a Carthusian, expressing a profound intuition: "To know is simply to *be* more, more fully, more truly. To know is to be enriched with the very being of things, allowing them to be what they are." No, to know is neither to consume things nor to digest them. On the contrary, it is to contribute to their advancement, by communicating to them a second existence. Once, they exist in themselves, for themselves. A second time, they exist for the knower and in the knower.

We understand why the philosophers who have spoken best of knowledge have done so by employing the verb "to be." To know is to "be" in some sort "all that is," said Aristotle, as we have seen. The contemplative monk we have quoted exalted the value of knowledge in these terms: "The intellect, essential gentleness, respects beings absolutely, and thereby finds itself the heir of their virtues."

It is correct, then, to strike an analogy between the soul of plants that composes their organs for the purpose of flowers, and the human soul, which composes its organs in order to "blossom in the flower of all that is."[2] Aristotle had already observed: "Vision, in the human being, produces no work alongside itself. Vision is attained in the viewer, as contemplation in the person contemplating," as the plant is perfected in its flower (*Metaphysics* 1050a.23–25).

3

Knowledge Gathers All Things in the Soul

A sanctuary of infinite breadth . . . .
                                        —St. Augustine

ST. AUGUSTINE, THAT GENIUS of introspection, questioned himself on the fact that what the knower sees within, receives within, are not images of things, but the things themselves. And he is even more astonished that, without taking leave of itself, the soul nevertheless attains the things themselves, "with the dimensions that are perceived by my regard without" (Augustine, *Confessions* 10.10). With these observations, St. Augustine moves from the mind to the very heart of the mystery of knowledge in a single bound. Lest we clumsily miss the mystery, we must assert that, for one and the same unique reality, there are two different manners of existence. These mountains, these waves, these rivers surely exist outside of my consciousness. This is why they receive the name of "things." It is no longer a humdrum term. What it means is that these realities are fully independent of consciousness, and fully responsible for what they do. Still, these same mountains, these same waves, these same rivers also exist, and even more, in the consciousness. And so they are called "objects." The word comes from the Latin *ob*, which means "athwart," "across the path of," and *jacere*, "to place." In order to be known, all realities are placed "within," and at the same time "in front of," consciousness.

Knowledge is surely paradoxical. In order to conceptualize the "miraculous" power of this act, we must say that the reality of the *thing* takes on, within the knower, the "existence" of an *object*. Let us see in this word the humble effort of the mind to describe, as well as possible, what actually occurs in such an act. How could we define in any other way the extraordinary privilege possessed by "knowers" in causing to "exist" within them any reality you please, without exception? And spontaneously, it is indeed the reality in itself that we regard within ourselves, and not a photo album! St. Augustine is right: What the soul stores are not the images of realities but the realities themselves. After all, it is my mother whom I see, my mother herself in me, she who is no longer. I am not looking at her photograph.

Besides my own individual existence, I also exist in things. And things, besides their own existence, receive as well the existence of objects. Together, consciousness and things "super-exist." The contemplative we have already quoted expresses this paradox felicitously. "Nothing is more evident than the fact that we live at once our own act and that of a limitless quantity of objects. We actualize ourselves by receiving the *objective reality* of an indefinite quantity of extraneous acts." Here once more we meet Heraclitus's declaration: that we shall never find the floor of the soul. This is true precisely because of the act of knowledge, which makes of the human soul "a sanctuary of infinite breadth. The mind is too wide to keep to itself" (*Confessions* 10.8).

4

Our Body Is Modeled by the Soul to Reflect the Things That Are Outside Ourselves

The body is the work of the soul. It is its expression, and its prolongation in the domain of matter.

—Paul Claudel

THE FOREGOING CHAPTERS sought to establish that the body exists for the purpose of the soul. It is in studying the structure of the organs that compose the body that we discover for what end the soul builds them. They reveal, we might say, the unconscious intentions of the soul that invents them.

Organs like the eye, the ear, the nose, the mouth present themselves in the form of receptors. They are obviously fashioned to receive the messages that come from things in the world. They are so many "open doors," where qualities, the shapes of sensible things, enter the soul. They are so many recesses in which the soul accumulates the numberless objects offered by the world. Thus, we "toss" a whole, delicious "salad" within our consciousness.

The organs of the senses (like the other organs, for that matter—legs, arms, hands) are not tools "screwed on" from the

11

outside on an already existing soul. Just the opposite: it is the soul itself that makes them "grow into a body" to attain its end. Now, the organs of the senses, of themselves, are directed to knowledge. Who could doubt it? St. Augustine interrogates them on the part they have in consciousness and invites them to respond. Here is what they say: The eyes say, "If things have a color, it is we who have brought these messages." The ears say: "If they resonate, it is from us that their revelations come." The nostrils say: "If they have a scent, it is through us that they have passed" (*Confessions* 10.10).

This dramatic presentation, very much in the style of Augustine, is an unsurpassably clear statement of the raison d'être of the organs of the senses. The soul *sends* them forth, as its tools of perception, of apprehension. It is by them that the soul establishes its grasp of the rich interest prepared for it in the world.

For example, let us cite these lines of Paul Claudel, describing, in this perspective, the organ of the eye.

> This type of burgeoning thing, these buds, translucent, these two globes charged with exquisite devices, filling the double alcove of the skull and contriving to be capable of sallying forth in all directions, this double receptive sun, by which one communes with all that is light without! It is as if the need to see had made the eye, the eye the face, the face the head, and the head this flexible neck![3]

Were we to repeat similar descriptions for the rest of the organs of sense, we should realize how correct it is to say, with Aristotle, "The *whole* body exists for the soul" (*The Parts of Animals* 64b.13). We would also realize how incorrect it is to say, for example, "The soul is *in* the body, as if it were imprisoned there by it." No, the body is in no way an obstacle to the soul. It is its indispensable "tool."

There is more. It is in order to ensure a more complete

reception of things that, within the body, the soul effects the "growing" of the brain. In this organ, of an incredible complexity, the soul determines zones that will serve for the exercise of the internal senses—the "common sense," the imagination, the memory. These cerebral areas have, as it were, the duty of further refining the data of the external senses, of unifying them, of setting them in relation with other data distributed through space and time. All of this in order to store, more vastly and more lengthily in time, the "precious universe"—the universe not only in "our knowing hands," but within the very body, in the "spacious palaces of imagination, and the warehouses of memory."

5

The "Common Sense" Thrusts the Data of the External Senses More Profoundly into Consciousness

The senses have a dark, speculative value.

—Jacques Maritain

EVERYTHING ABOUT A PLANT, in all of its parts—roots, stem, leaves—all is for the purpose of the blossom and the fruit, which these parts toil to form. The flower and fruit are the true causes of the labor produced by the seed. We must say the same thing of the human soul in the genesis of its body. If the soul gives itself the organs of five external senses, it is for the purpose of arriving at knowledge. Jacques Maritain calls knowledge "the blossoming of my being in the flower of all that is."[4]

The entry of things, with their sensible qualities and their contours, into knowledge represents the first step toward this "spiritual blossoming." Let us speak, now, of the following step, the one in which the human soul constructs—within its body—the organ of the brain. In the brain, the soul creates the zones of reception whose purpose is to "interiorize" the data of the external senses. An anatomical section of the human brain shows the localizations of three internal senses: the

14

"common sense," the imagination, and the memory. Through these three faculties, the sensible data received from the outside are subjected to further elaboration. And this elaboration prepares the sensible object for a reading of this piece of reality by the intellect.

We shall speak first of the internal sense that Aristotle calls the "common sense." We must not understand this expression as if it meant "good sense," or the quality of dealing "sensibly" in our affairs. To avoid this equivocation, moderns call this sense "gnosis." We are dealing this time with an internal sense, since it is connected to an area of the brain.

All sensations delivered by the external senses converge on this sense in order to be synthesized. Aristotle himself discovered this faculty of integration on the basis of very simple experiments. If when I view the yellow color of a lemon I am automatically put in mind of its acidity, this very fact implies that these two sensible data have been previously joined in a single sense that cannot but be internal. The soul builds in the brain a tool whose task it is to collect and integrate the multiplicity of pieces of information that *in themselves* are disparate. *Of themselves,* after all, colors, odors, tastes, being qualitatively distinct, do not "cross-check"—indeed, they oppose one another. A part of the brain, built by the soul, receives a unifying faculty that forms, of all of these data, one and the same object.

This function of unification has great importance. The common sense, which exercises it, provides the object of the senses with a consistency of its own on the level of sensibility. The various impressions, colors, tastes, and odors are polarized toward one and the same object and cease to be purely "subjective." What the sensibility knows, then, is like a sketch of what the intellect will call the "being" of the thing.

There also begins, for the knowing "subject"—that in which

an action or attribute inheres—a consciousness of itself. Thanks to this internal sense, knowers experience that they see, that they understand. It is not yet formally a "self-awareness," but it is a consciousness of our operations precisely as ours. It is impossible for an external sense, attached to an organ, to reflect upon itself. But the common sense, gathering the objects and sensations of the external senses, knows them as its own.

The "common sense," then, performs two typical functions. Of the teeming sensory data, it founds a cohesion in one and the same object, despite their disparity. On the other hand, in the presence of this object, it contributes to, shall we say, a "foreshadowed" consciousness of self. In the performance of these two functions, the soul accomplishes a decisive step toward an act of perfect knowledge. The soul prepares itself to receive, on the level of sensibility, things in their own consistency, and thus to allow them their objective independence. The soul is thus prepared to receive the actual being of things, and in letting them be what they are. Now we can say, in all truth, that, in this knowledge, the soul realizes its specific flowering: ". . . Blossoming in the flower of all that is." It is in the common sense that, first, the "dark, speculative value" of the senses is revealed.

6

On the Path from Sensibility to Mind: The Imagination Partakes of Both

The imagination is the eye of the soul.

−J. Joubert

THE KNOWLEDGE OF ALL THINGS is sought by the human soul as the seed seeks its flower. That to which the soul tends, the contemplative philosopher calls "the universal rose." It is surely true that, among the animals, the human being is distinguished by the faculty of receiving in her mind an unlimited quantity of objects. This quasi-infinite faculty of openness is partially provided by the imagination, which "gives its all" to achieve this effect.

It is the marvelous prerogative of the imagination to be able to render present to awareness once more objects now physically absent. St. Augustine celebrates the immense treasure over which the imagination keeps watch: "There we find countless images, brought in by every sort of perception" (*Confessions* 10.8).

Besides its faculty of conservation of forms, what is admirable in the imagination is its extraordinary spontaneity. This enables it to contemplate anew an indefinite number of

things that, without it, would founder forever in the unconscious. St. Augustine, still on the subject of the life of the consciousness of imagination, writes:

> In vain do I rest in darkness and silence. I can represent the col-
> ors, as I please, distinguish white from black, and all of the
> other colors from one another. . . . I evoke the impressions
> introduced and stored up in me by my other senses as I please.
> I distinguish the perfume of the lily from that of violets, with-
> out smelling a flower. I can prefer honey to wine sauce, the
> smooth to the rough, without tasting anything or touching any-
> thing. (*Confessions* 10.8)

What we must emphasize is the "intentional" character of
images. The word "intentional" evokes the *realistic* nature of
the image. When the knower produces an image, for the purpose of re-presenting an absent thing, it is not the image he
sees, but the thing, made present. It is not the images of things
that we know, but things in images. The images are deleted
before the object. They place the awareness in immediate relationship with the things themselves.

The image permits the thing to take on a *new mode of existence*. And for that reason the knower has no need of emerging spatially from herself into the outer world. It is rather the
outer world that is suddenly present in the soul, but not without the soul's having given it a new existence. The beings that
existed outside the soul are summoned within by the soul:

> Here it is that I have at my command the sky, the earth, the sea,
> and all of the sensations that I have managed to have of them,
> save the ones I have forgotten. And how could I speak of the
> mountains, waves, rivers, and stars that I have seen, unless I saw
> them interiorly, in my memory, in the dimensions that my eyes
> perceived outside? (*Confessions* 10.8)

We notice, in this text, the dialectic of "within and without"
that Augustine uses to express the mystery of the imaging
consciousness.

With this psychic vitality, its dumbfounding spontaneity, and its intentionality, the imagination attaches to the brain. In a fraction of a second, I have Paris in me, I have my mother in me—and yet she left this world more than thirty years ago! Still, my imagination has need of the body. It is in order to endow itself with such a power of awareness that the soul has built, this time in the brain itself, physical tools of an extreme delicacy: "These brain images go far beyond the mere zones of sensory reception, and involve an immense extent of the brain."[5] Once more we must say: "The human soul has need of the body." With it and by it, the soul accomplishes marvels!

7

Thanks to the Memory, the Human Soul Begins to Breathe above Time

I see all of the past growing within me.
—Apollinaris

THE IMAGINATION ENJOYS the collaboration of another internal faculty; and thanks to it, consciousness is consolidated. We shall now speak of the memory. Amidst the throng of objects that the imagination resurrects thanks to the memory, the subject of knowledge—the knower—takes root and grows.

The huge river of sensations and images is not completely lost in the unconscious. Even if the majority of the objects known will never again come to awareness, the memory can draw a considerable number of them from this overwhelming trove. The memory has the power to delve them up from the sands of oblivion and haul them to the surface. It also creates among them continuities, units that constitute what Bergson called "duration." Duration, to Bergson, was like the shadow of being, cast through the soul's time.

Let us pause to contemplate this "miraculous" power of the human soul—the power to recover whole sections of our life, to make them exist anew, not in their natural being, of course, but in this existence that we have called "intentional." One could think the past buried forever—yet suddenly it is rendered present, in this "immaterial" existence.

Besides, the act of memory bestows on the knower the capacity to "see" himself or herself in the past, as the images of the past ascend once more to consciousness. The return of the past through images is the condition for the act of memory, but it is the memory that formally introduces into this psychic continuity the structure of relations "according to priority and posteriority." The proper object of the memory is time, with its triple structure: past, present, and future. But it is the past as such that the memory records.

"In myself, I see all of the past growing large." Thanks to the memory, I can say: Eight years ago I went to Reunion Island on a teaching assignment. But before that I had already executed a teaching assignment for thirty years in a high school in Switzerland. St. Thomas Aquinas is precise: the task of the memory is to *sentire tempus*–to "sense," or "feel" time. We could likewise translate the expression as "to have the internal sensation of time."

To effect continuity at the heart of past actions—to create, therefore, a duration, to build a whole—such is the first office of the memory. And in carrying it out, the memory cooperates in the creation of the "psychological 'I.'" St. Augustine, once more, has said it:

> It is in the immense palace of my memory that I meet myself, that I remember myself, what I have done, the moment and place that I have done it, the affective dispositions in which I was at that moment and in that place, as I did what I did. (Augustine, *Confessions* 10.8)

And of course it is true that I cannot recover acts of my past life without seeing myself involved in them. Remembering my past actions is seeing "me" teaching, climbing mountains, flying over oceans. The continuity of my life, set in a sequence of images, corresponds necessarily to the continuity of *my* existence, and hence to "myself": "I find myself," said St. Augustine. Without the memory, I would have but an instantaneous, "punctual" (from the Latin *punctum*, "point") existence. My existence would be the next thing to nothing, deprived as it would be of continuity, of permanence. Under the light of consciousness, the memory gathers in the identity of my being. I notice that I am a successive totality. The memory, then, is the special tool of consciousness of self. A purely instantaneous consciousness, made only of a flash of awareness, would border on unconsciousness.

Hence, the memory sets the knower as a subject facing an object. Obviously, without both poles—subject and object—there is no knowledge. But here again we must emphasize that, in order for the act of memory to occur, physiological conditions must intervene. Even if the question of brain localizations is still open as to the precise zones assigned to each respective brain function, it is the organ that is localized. The act of knowing is purely psychic to that organ. The brain alone, let us be clear, is surely the condition of external sensible knowing, as well as that of internal sensible knowing. Here we find again the truth that is the whole prop and stay of our presentation in part 1 of this book: "The body is the work of the soul."

As we come to the end of this chapter, there is something upon which we must insist, in order that the reader understand the role of the memory exactly. We must never lose sight of the fact that this faculty preserves the past, but only as an object of knowing. Through the memory, the past is made present, surely—but only in terms of "intentional" existence. It is likewise true that, by reason of intentional existence, it is the past itself that is known, and not the image of the past as image. But this does not militate against the fact that the past, in its physical, material reality, exists no longer. And that is why we can say that, thanks to the memory, it is given to us to be not only what we are but also what we no longer are!

Conclusion of Part 1

I N ORDER TO PENETRATE somewhat the mystery of the human soul, we have begun by considering its very first labor. We have contemplated it at work when, for its future operations, it builds its own tools, that is, its organs. We have especially contemplated those that it prepares for its most specific activity: *knowing*.

We should have to be able to follow at length, as does the physiologist, the intelligent work of nature: the polishing of the lens of the eye, the construction of a photographic darkroom, the excavation and formation in the skull of cavities for the ear, the nose, the mouth. It is obvious now that the internal "principle" of the human being, like the blossom and the bird, for that matter, are under the direction of a "manufacturing idea." Claude Bernard, at all events, centuries after Aristotle, adopted this same appellation: *directive idea,* or *entelechy.*

But this same vital principle is more than the manufacturer of its own tools. It is also endowed with the power of applying them. And it is under this precise angle that it has the right to be called, as well, "soul." The purpose of this appellation is to indicate the *idea* of the body, which this constructive principle instills in its organs—that is, the organs of its external and internal senses, the power to grasp sensible qualities, the

24

shapes that the body of nature offers them to the infinite. The human soul could borrow the saying of the poet:

> I have spread the vast net of my knowing,
> like the musical phrase
> that begins with the horns,
> spreads to the woodwinds,
> and little by little,
> pervades the depths of the orchestra.[6]

Part 2

Human Beings:
Their Intellectual Life

*The intellect, essential gentleness,
respects beings absolutely.*

—A Carthusian

8

The Faculty of the Invisible

*If the dew sparkles in the sun, how much the more
does the shining human substantial soul sparkle
in the intelligible ray!*

—Paul Claudel

THE ORGANS OF THE EXTERNAL and internal senses, of
which the human soul constitutes its body, have the function of gathering up the infinite wealth of the sensible qualities offered by the things of nature. But what these senses
know in these things is only a part. Besides sensible objects, a
more precious object yet remains to be grasped. But for this
there must be another faculty than the senses. This other faculty receives the name of "intellect." And it is of this that we
must now speak.

The word "intellect" is composed of two Latin words: *intus,*
meaning "within," and *lectus,* which denotes the act of "gathering," hence also of "reading." To give to a faculty of knowing the name of intellect implies that, in the things that the
senses present to awareness, there is a "within" that they do
not grasp. And since only the intellect can understand this
object, it receives the name of *intelligible.* What are we to say
of it?

We can say what the intelligible is by reflecting on the same
question as was asked apropos of what the senses furnish to

the soul. That question is still the same as every person of every time of life asks the data of the senses. The intellect asks, concerning what the senses grasp in things . . . *What is it?*

Does a like question not imply that, in everything in nature, besides what the senses know, there remains an unknown? Otherwise the question What is it? would be absurd. The question reveals that, besides the senses, there is in the human soul a faculty to which it is proper to seek this unknown. But first let us pause to examine the question itself.

To "question" comes from the Latin *quaerere*. This verb means in Latin "to seek." The human soul seeks in things an object to know that the senses have not delivered to it. This object faces another faculty. The object is hidden from the senses: it is "within" the thing. We do very well to call it the "intelligible," and to give to the faculty that "seeks" it the name of "intellect." Let us note at once that this object must have a great breadth, since we ask the question What is it? about everything that is.

9

The Intellect and Its Hidden Domain

*As there are color-blind persons, . . . so also
there are being-blind persons.*

—Martin Heidegger

IN ORDER TO GO DEEPER into this object that the intellect
seeks in sensible things, we propose the following route:

About everything that the senses present, one question is
invariably asked: What is it? And so there must be something
else to know in what, nevertheless, enters us by the senses.
This question, the first of all questions, ceaselessly repeated,
must not only be mentioned, it must be plumbed, scrutinized.

In asking the question What is it? the intellect reveals that
it sees at once an object for it in the sensible datum itself. It
has glimpsed this object, then, but it cannot pierce it all at
once. It has apprehended it; it has not *understood* it. It seeks to
"gather up" this object that is there for it. This is the second
meaning of the word "intellect": to plumb the interior of its
proper object. In asking this question, and asking it again, the
intellect would like to take it entirely within it!

Can we call this object of the intellect by its name? Surely
we can. The name is in the question itself. Is there not, in this
question, the verb "to be"? To ask the question What *is* it? is,

31

in a way, to admit that, in every sensible thing, the intellect seeks "being." But to seek being in a thing of nature is to seek "what holds together" the organs of a thing and causes its specific actions and qualities. To seek the being of a flower is to seek the reason which, within it, brings it about that its roots, stem, leaves, blossoms, and specific operations all "hold together" in a profound oneness. The intellect sees at once that, in a daisy, for example, there is a unifying principle *within* what it presents to the senses.

We recall that in chapter 1 we had to recognize that, within a body in the course of formation, there is a "directive idea." This idea is the reason for the edifice of any living body, plant, animal, or person. Now, Claude Bernard calls this principle an "invisible guide." Invisible for whom? Certainly invisible to the senses, even to the senses using their most refined tools of experience. This "invisible guide," then, is the "directive idea," of which the intellect sees the existence at once, but whose nature it would like further to penetrate.

The being of things? It shows and hides itself at the same time. Here we can borrow Heideggerian terminology: Being is what is nearest.[1] It is before our eyes, our ears; it is under our hand. And yet it is the farthest away. The intellect sees it at once, but it would like to "catch" this element so invisible to the senses, that is also partially invisible to it, the intellect. By asking of everything the question What *is* it? the intellect reveals that its proper object is the *being* of things.

10

The Intellect, Essential Gentleness

Water apprehends water, mind inhales essence.
                                    —Paul Claudel

THE INTELLECT SEEKS THE BEING of things. The philosopher also employs the expression "The intellect seeks *essences.*" Why this word? In order to understand it, we must have recourse once more to etymology. "Essence" comes from the Latin *esse,* which means "exist." In the word "essence," the ear perceives the word *esse.* To seek the essence of things is to seek the reason for their existence. This reason is precisely the "directive idea" of which we have spoken in the preceding chapter. To find the directive idea of a thing is to say why it exists as it exists.

The reason for existence—this is what precisely none of the senses is concerned with. The senses record facts. But they are precisely incapable of grasping in them a right to existence. The right of a thing to exist, its legitimacy in the face of reason, so many expressions that show where the interest is to be found that the intellect brings to sensible realities—nothing of this is the object of the senses. To seek the essence of things is to seek what justifies them in maintaining themselves outside of nothingness and in maintaining itself in them. It is neither to use them nor to consume them. To seek to know them in themselves and for themselves is to love them purely and to devote energy and time to them. A contemplative says this with a rare felicity of expression: "The intellect, essential gentleness, respects beings absolutely."

For a fair estimate of love for things in someone who seeks to understand their essence, one must read *Nausea,* by Jean-Paul Sartre. Essences? He despises them. He repudiates them. He applies all of his genius to flatten them out, to violate them, precisely by depriving things of all raison d'être. The result is that he dares to treat them as "ignoble marmelade."

What a contrast, for example, with the effort of the scientist concerned to draw up inventories of the properties of the bodies of nature! The properties scientists list do not yet give them the essence in itself. But, as the poet says, they inhale this essence present at the heart of properties—precisely their raison d'être.We need only think of the long, patient days laboratories devote to the observation and description of the bodies of nature.

We may say as much of the painter and the poet. By other routes than those of the scientist, they too observe and contemplate the things of the sensible world. What they seek to capture is the savor of a singular essence. In revealing their analogy, the poet manages to plumb its depth. Let us hear the poet speaking of the cypress.

> Like a shepherd in the fog,
> Counting and counting again his sheep,
> Anxiety in his heart
> Under his meager cape.[2]

Poets and painters lurk and watch—watch things, waiting for their prey! In a long, twenty-four-stanza poem, Rainer Maria Rilke sings the mystery of the rose, of its perfume subtle as spirit.

Tell me, rose, whence it is
That, shut within thee,
Thy slow essence imposes
On this space, in prose,
All of these airy transports![3]

Spontaneously, in these lines, we notice that the poet adopts the very vocabulary of the philosopher: the "slow essence" of the rose!

11

To Blossom in the Flower of All That Is

As light to the eye, and sound to the ear,
So is each and every thing
to the analysis of the intellect.

—Paul Claudel

A T THIS POINT IN OUR EXPOSITION, it will be well to examine the steps of the expedition of thought.

We have undertaken to penetrate the mystery of the human soul. How are we to go about it? Here, we assure you, we must contemplate it first in its very first labor, that of building its body. Why does it begin by building itself a bundle of organs? Why eyes, ears, a nose, a mouth? Clearly, these are tools destined to grasp the rich booty of the qualities offered by the bodies of nature. It is precisely to this end that the soul arranges these organs on the surface of the body. Then it builds the brain within, where the data of the external senses are taken up and developed by imagination and memory.

Now, there is no escaping it: the external and internal senses do not exhaust all that is to be known in things. We discover the proof of this in the fact that the data of the senses leave the intellect hungry. Otherwise, why would it feel the need to ask the question What is it? Is this not a sign that, in the data of the senses, there is an object to be known that the senses cannot reveal? What is this object?

The intellect formulates the nature of this object, which it asks to know, in the very question. The verb in this question is an indicative form, "is," of the verb "to be." Now, etymologically, "is" means "maintains itself in itself." Therefore one can ask the question in these terms as well: "This hyacinth before me—how can it 'maintain itself' in itself?" What the intellect seeks is the architectural idea at work in this flower. What the intellect desires to know is the essence: that which gives this flower the right to exist.

The intellect "inhales essence," said Paul Claudel. It is so eager to gather up this "scintilla of light" that attracts it in the depths of things. Only a contemplative is able to experience to the depths of the soul a "silent enthusiasm" before the passion of the intelligence:

> The intellect awakens the day it wonders what a being is. It asks this question alone. It finds the answer in the purest, most immediate part of itself. It perceives that it knows one thing. By its nature, the intellect only knows something under the light of its reason for being, and what of itself has a relationship with being. And in the simplicity of this point, on which, as if on an invisible ruby, it balances the universe, it can already perceive the divine oneness whose vision is promised to it.

And so the intelligence is made to know being. But being is surely what basically belongs to all things. Yes, it is surely in order to be able to seize this "intelligible" that the soul has worked to give itself the body it has and thereby, one day, to "blossom in the flower of all that is."

12

"A Light Deriving from the Highest Sun"

You see, the poet has a kind of spiritual energy of a special nature.

—Paul Valéry

THERE IS, IN HUMAN BEINGS, a faculty of knowledge that separates them from the animals absolutely. The datum of which the intellect goes in quest in the senses is invisible to the senses. And yet, Aristotle says, pithily: "It is in sensible forms that intelligibles exist" (*On the Soul* 3.432a.5).

First, what the soul needs is a light shining upon it. One can only see in the light. "Color is visible only with the light of the sun. It is only in light that the color of any object is perceived" (*On the Soul* 2.418b.2–5).

There will also be need of a light, then, for the intellect to be able to see this part of the knowable within things. True, this light can only be analogous to that of the sun. It is a spiritual, immaterial light. And it emanates from the soul itself. "Necessarily found in the soul," Aristotle observes, "will be a sort of state analogous to light" (*On the Soul* 3.430a.18).

These reflections suggest the following analogy. Just as the light of the sun gives colors, heretofore invisible, to be perceived, so the light of the soul gives the intelligible, hidden from the senses, to become recognizable. Aristotle calls this source of light the *agent intellect* (*On the Soul* 3.430a.15). It is like a point of spiritual light radiating upon the soul.

Jacques Maritain has described this inner sun of the soul in terms of great inner sensitivity. "We possess within us," he says, "the 'illuminating intellect,' a spiritual sun ceaselessly shining, activating everything in the intelligence, its light arousing all of our ideas in us and penetrating with its energy all of the operations of our mind. This original source of light remains invisible to us, hidden in the unconscious part of the mind."[4]

It is thanks to this light, then, which the soul bears within it, this light ever activating, that the "intelligible glows" at the heart of things!

13

Like a Hand, the Intellect Gathers Being at the Heart of Things

By space, the universe embraces me all around, and overwhelms like a point. By thought, I comprehend the universe.

—Pascal

T HE HUMAN SOUL POSSESSES the power to bring to light that which is hidden in the things of nature. The soul, in order to respond to this illuminating faculty, associates to it the faculty of gathering what it strives to know.

The question springing up from this faculty, What is it? is the sign of the fundamental, restless aspiration in a person's soul, the desire to understand, in each thing, its being, its essence. To take the measure of this desire to know, we need only hear the numberless, insistent questions of a child! At birth, the intellect within us is like "a slate on which nothing has yet been written" (Aristotle, *On the Soul* 3.430a.1). However, this celebrated comparison of Aristotle's leaves an essential aspect unelucidated. A blank slate is but pure passivity, pure waiting. By contrast, the child's intellect is a constant, fierce desire to know. It is in potency to know, but also eager to know. The illuminative intellect, with its intelligible beam, provokes its arousal. Its sleep is watchful, like that of the bride in the Song of Songs!

By our sensations, relayed by imagination and memory as if by channels, the being of things enters into the soul incognito. The intellect, waiting to know it, seizes this being. It is once more by a comparison that Aristotle illustrates this process. "The knowing soul," he says, "is analogous to the hand. Just as the hand is the instrument of instruments, so also the intellect is the form of forms, further forming the sensations presented by the senses" (*On the Soul* 432a.1–3).

Let us interpret Aristotle's comparison. Using the senses as tools, the human soul absorbs what is most profound in things, their being. We may also call it their directive idea, the formative idea that makes them maintain themselves as they are—in the form of a daisy, for example, in the form of a jonquil. To begin with, these forms of being, these essences, are seen but are not penetrated. Then the illuminative intellect sheds its ray of light on the sensible datum, and this object, as yet hidden, is grasped by that part of the intellect that desires to know, the part that asks questions. This part acts like a hand taking something for itself. It is the hand of the soul. It causes to enter into the soul the "idea" of the thing, the substantial form of the thing. It enters into the intellect and becomes a seed of light there. The intelligence envelops it, in some sort, in a new existence. And in this wise the human soul grows rich in the very being of things. Such is the gentleness of this act: to take within it the being of another thing while nevertheless letting it be what it is in itself! Thanks to this new existence, which it gives to the things within it, the soul is born, in a way, to that which it is not—"altogether infiltrated with this other being."[5]

When Aristotle's most penetrating commentator, St. Thomas Aquinas, evokes the mystery of knowing, his enthusiasm betrays itself. Let us conclude with what he writes:

Thanks to the intellect, the following occurs. The property of a thing, the very same, now finds itself in another thing. Such is the property of the knower as such. Inasmuch as the knower knows, the known *in a certain manner exists in the* [knower]. . . . And according to that mode . . . it is possible that, in one particular being, there exist the [properties] of the entire universe. (*De Veritate,* q. 2, a. 2)

Yes, the entire universe in this "thinking reed" (Pascal, *Pensées,* 348). Yes, the human being becomes the seat of "its blossoming in the flower of all that is."

14

The Intellect Discovers Existence

Like the great poor, being is hidden in light.

—Jacques Maritain

W HAT HAS BEEN SAID up until now of the manner in which the intelligence acquires knowledge of being in things, concerns only the *essence,* the nature, of this being. After all, when, apropos of a natural body, one asks, "What is it?" it is its essence that is being asked about. But when the answer, for example, is, "This tree is an oak," the intellect not only declares the nature of this tree; it also declares that it *exists.* It declares that it maintains itself above nothingness and outside of the knower.

There is a great difference between performing an "oak" project, becoming an oak—that is, growing in conformity with the idea of an oak—and performing the act of maintaining oneself outside of nothingness. These two acts are performed along different lines. It must be admitted that most of the time the intellect does not seem particularly concerned with existence. There is a great deal of truth in Sartre's observation, "Usually existence hides. It is all around us. . . . One cannot pronounce many words without speaking of it [by saying "is," or "am," or the like], and finally, one never touches it."[6]

And yet existence is the content of the verb "to be," at the heart of a judgment. Thus, existence has at first entered into the soul incognito. The senses cannot see it, any more than they can see essence. Existence has entered in, but "masked," as it were, in the shock that the senses receive in the activity of bodies upon them. Sensations are called "impressions" because they exert pressure *on* the senses, *against* the senses. But it is the intelligence that receives existence through the ministry of the senses, that pronounces upon it at the heart of the judgment: "This tree *is* an oak."

Notice, however: while existence is enunciated in every judgment, nevertheless, usually it is not "seen" for itself. At the same time, everything is prepared for such an intuition to be had. When something occurs that sets it in relief, existence casts the intellect into an actual metaphysical experience. "It is on the occasion of some individual reality, grasped in its pure singularity, that the intellectual intuition of being is produced."[7] But most of the time existence is "like the great poor, hidden in the light."[8]

The day arrives when the intellect is no longer "blind" to existence. It sees that the act of maintaining oneself above nothingness is a very different thing from the act of realizing an oak project, or a rose project. Then it sees that these two acts that compose being compose it according to an innumerable diversity of species and individuals. And suddenly the intellect gazes out upon an unlimited, infinite domain. "The essential thing is to have seen that existence is not a simple empirical fact, but a primordial datum for the mind itself, delivering to it an infinite supra-observable field."[9]

Conclusion of Part 2

"A FINE WAY TO KNOW the soul is to regard the body. . . ." This was the theme of the first part of this book. We have followed Paul Claudel's advice, for he continues: ". . . and, from our external equipment of perception and apprehension, to conclude to internal agents that use them and direct them after having built them."[10] And so the soul first devotes itself to seeing in and by the body, which it has put together to use for its own purposes.

The case is the same, for that matter, when we seek to know the soul of a flower. We must contemplate the vital energy that sets the blossom of the daisy at the tip of a delicate green stem and gives it a chalice of pure whiteness to gather there the sparkling gold of its heart. Then it stops, in "this secret that draws it." It is also true for the soul of the blackbird. After all, it is its soul that it opens to us when it sings with all its body! "The blackbird suddenly sang. . . . I felt immediately that its song absorbed it completely, preventing it from seeing anything and making it forget everything in the world. I said to myself that perhaps at that moment it was closing its eyes."[11]

What our part 2 has tried to say is this. The human soul builds the organs of the external and internal senses to make for itself instruments of knowledge. In the sensible forms brought by the senses, the intelligence can "read" the being of things. We have sought to show how the intellect feels attracted, so to speak, toward something deeper, but something found in the sensible qualities, shapes, and operations of the bodies of nature. The intellect "questions"—that is, seeks to grasp hold of an object that is for itself alone!

Here we must cite the observation with which Aristotle opens his *Metaphysics.* "Every person has by nature the desire to know" (1.980a.1). To know, and that is all! To know apart from all utility. And to know everything. We have found this desire in the ever-repeated question, What is it? There the intellect reveals its entire nature. And its nature consists in the desire to know the being of everything. This is why the human soul gives itself the organs of the external and internal senses: to "blossom in the flower of all that is"! If we ask the human soul about its nature, it replies: "I am in every person as the seed that, with its light, bends its efforts that all things be born again in me, and that I, too, be born with them." Joubert said, "The intellect is the blooming, the complete development of the seed of the human plant."[12]

"**A**s for me, I say that there is nothing in nature made without design, or word addressed to the human being. And as light to the eye, and sound to the ear, so is each and every thing to the analysis of the intellect."[13]

Part 3

Human Beings: Their Affective Life

The senses are places where the soul has pleasures and pains.

—J. Joubert

15

The Body and the Affective Life of the Human Soul

*Light, queen of colors, . . . slips toward me,
in a thousand ways, caresses me. . . . If it is taken
from us, we desire it, we seek it, and if its absence is
prolonged, our soul is all sorrowful.*

—St. Augustine

IN ORDER TO UNDERSTAND the nature of the human soul,
one must first consider its body. The soul toils as the seed.
But it is not branches and leaves that it grows; it is external
and internal senses. It is correct to say, then, that the very first
concern of the human soul is to prepare instruments of knowing. There, we have asserted, is its first "finality," its first end
and aim.

In this third part, we wish to show that these same organs
have been grown by the soul to serve its affective life, as well.
On this point we find Aristotle once more. In his treatise *On
the Soul,* he writes: "Where there is sensation, there is also pain
and pleasure, and where there is pain and pleasure, there is
necessarily appetite. Thus it is in the sphere of the external
senses, indeed, . . ." (2.413b.24) that the first affects of the soul
awaken. The soul bestows sensory organs upon itself not only
in order to know but also in order to enter into affective relation with things.

Apropos of human activity, Aristotle makes this observation: "It would seem that all of the affections of the soul come with a body—courage, gentleness, fear, pity, daring, and joy, love, and hatred. At the same time, after all, as these determinations are produced, the body experiences a modification" (*On the Soul* 1.403a.15–16). With this declaration, Aristotle betakes himself to his treatise on the passions, as conjoint expressions of the soul and the body. Pain transforms the face. Anger hardens its features, warps them, colors them. It would be easy to show, for each of the passions, their specific corporeal accompaniment. Certain painters, like Daumier, have devoted their art to imprinting on the body the revelatory deformations of the sentiments, the emotions, the passions. Or we may think of Hieronymus Bosch, his painting of the *Carrying of the Cross*. While Christ presents a face filled with a gentle life, those who surround him, his enemies, wear hideous faces, with sadistic creases. We may think of Rouault's personages, their faces swollen with pridefulness and lust. Beyond any doubt, it is for its affective life, as well, that the soul grows sensory organs and gives itself the body it has.

The affective life of the soul can be caught in these movements at once psychic and physical. The soul, then, as Montaigne said, is "situated at the seam of mind and body." And it is by reason of its repercussions on the body, on its organs, that we are able to contemplate the human soul in its "passions." Why this word? The term "passion" has its origin in the Latin verb *pati*, "to suffer," "to undergo." Simultaneously and immediately, as soon as there is an affection of anger, there is a frown on the face. Certain psychologists have sought to establish a relation of "efficient causality" between them—to establish that the anger actually creases the facial features in an "expression of anger." Anger would first be felt, and then would receive a "bodily translation." Others say, on the contrary, that it is because I strike someone that I am in anger: "We feel sorrowful because we weep, fearful because we tremble."[1] But these theories fail to correspond to the facts. It is surely simpler to find, in the area of the passions, the Aristotelian distinction, and to say: the somatic reactions play the role of matter, and the psychic affect, the role of form.

What gives birth to the passions is the coefficient of goodness or noxiousness that things present. Goodness calls forth in the soul a "desiring faculty," as Aristotle calls it. Presented with good, the soul becomes basically "appetite," "love." Before sensible good and evil, the soul and body together enter upon a play of affective movements (Aristotle, *On the Soul* 3.431a9–11). Of all of the passions, without exception, the first "principle" or concrete foundation is "love" (433a.21)! But what is *love?*

16

The Soul's Emergence toward Things

To the angels, treetops may be roots, drinking the heavens.

—Rainer Maria Rilke

L OVE IS A PSYCHIC MOVEMENT that moves in an opposite direction to the movement of knowledge. As we have seen, knowing brings the object known into the soul on the basis of a resemblance. Under another mode of existence, the thing dwells in and enriches the knower—without, however, ceasing to continue to exist outside him or her. Love, for its part, calls the lover to emerge from self toward the object loved. The object loved also dwells in the lover, but under the form of an inclination, a value, bearing the lover forth to join the beloved in outward reality. The lover moves to unite with the beloved in the beloved's real existence. Lovers are literally "beside themselves"!

Here we shall follow the analyses of St. Thomas Aquinas, who presents love in the soul as a great star accompanied by three satellites.

1. Love is preceded by a connaturality between two beings. For there to be love between two beings, it is necessary for one of the two to possess a good of which the other is, as it were,

separated. If the plant "loves" water, it is because water is a part of its being. The plant is first separated from water as from its proper good. Then it tends necessarily toward it. The poet feels dynamically that, if a tree ascends toward the sky, one of the reasons is in order to find what it is lacking: air, sun, rain. The tree is made in order to "be together" with these things—for example, the poplar tree:

> At the summit of silence,
> Eager it drinks the sky
> At the source.[2]

2. Love now lives in a contract of suitability. Because two beings have need of each other, love sets them in motion toward each other. We say that they are "suitable" for each other. It is difficult to find the right words to suggest the fundamental dynamism of love. These separate things now seek each other. Each moves toward the other. The most convincing proof of this is the descent of the acacia! With its roots, it plunges more than thirty yards into the desert soil to seek, there, the water that awaits it:

> Trembling water, awaiting the ultimate assault of the roots.[3]

3. Last, love is consummated in relish or *delight.* When the union sought is realized, the lover reposes in the beloved. Then there is expansion, pleasure, fullness. Look at the face of the child who is eating a piece of delicious fruit. You are contemplating the very traits of love entered into possession of its good.

> Succulent apple, pear and banana,
> Green gooseberry . . .
> Behold the expression of all things—
> Life and death in someone's mouth. . . .
> And I doubt!
> But read it on the face of a child
> Tasting of it.[4]

As we see, love, the first principle of all of the passions, is born when, on the things of nature, the face of good appears. Good is the word given to any being capable of filling a void, of responding to a need. Correlatively, we see that all things are driven by an appetite for what is suitable to them, as if, before attaining it, they were separated from themselves. As Jacques Maritain observes: "What this reveals is a new face of being—a new mystery, consubstantial to being. . . . The good declares a merit—a glory, as well, and a joy."[5] And we also see how correct is St. Thomas's analysis of love as a passion of the soul. Yes, love is ever accompanied by connaturality, suitability, and delight (Thomas Aquinas, *Summa Theologiae* I–II, q. 26, a. 2).

17

The Play of the
Human Passions

*My charge is my love: wherever I am borne,
it is love that carries me.*

—St. Augustine

Love establishes among beings a type of specific
relation. St. Augustine compares it to a "charge," a weight,
that inclines and draws the lover toward the beloved. What
"carries" the lover outside herself is the desire to be united to
the beloved, in real existence. No form of being exists without
an inclination. It is because of this love inscribed in the nature
of each thing that each finds itself cast into adventure. Now,
human beings, because of the wealth of their nature, find
themselves borne off by three basic specific desires.

In the first place, there is *natural* love. It is called "natural"
because this tendency is pre-inscribed in its nature. And this
plays on the level of all of the faculties. There is a natural love
in the intellect, for example. Aristotle indicated it when he
said: "The human being has *by nature* the desire to know"
(*Metaphysics* 1.980a.21). Second, there is *sensible* love. This is a
tendency toward a thing whose goodness has been perceived
by one of the senses. While I am born with a natural inclination for nourishment, I am not come into the world with the
appetite for a particular brand of chocolate. The latter incli-

nation arises one day, after having had a taste experience recorded in the imagination! Finally, the human being has a *spiritual* appetite, a love born in consequence of a choice in which reason intervenes under the mode of a deliberation. This is voluntary appetite.

In this chapter we shall speak of the movements of the sensible appetite. The movements issuing from this love are called *passions.* The exercise of sight, hearing, smelling, taste, and touch is accompanied by an impression either of pleasure or of pain. At that moment, "impulsively," there are born in us sensible affects, accompanied by bodily modifications—that is, experienced passively. Anger, for example, is accompanied by a trembling of the muscles, by a coloration in the face.

While the passions are numberless in us, it has been possible to establish an order in this flow. First, they are grouped about two axes. Certain passions concern sensible good, others sensible evil. This is the first division. Next, they are classified into either the sphere of the "concupiscible" or that of the irascible. The former indicate the passions emerging from the instinct for pleasure. The latter are the passions arising from the instinct of aggressiveness.

The ancients drew up the table of the passions by organizing the movements of affectivity around two objects of appetite: sensible good and sensible evil. According to the conditions taken on by sensible good and evil, we have the passions presented in the chart on p. 57.

As we see, this classification demonstrates, in the human soul, on the level of its affectivity, eleven typical manners of reacting to sensible good and sensible evil. In each case, the psychic movement with which the soul is affected is accompanied by a bodily modification. Desire, hope, joy, sorrow, are translated by simultaneous movements in certain parts of the body, certain organs. At the same time, avenues of approach or of flight are established, of assault or withdrawal, of repose or of struggle. The play of the passions is a great keyboard of the human soul, interpreting what is experienced by its power of loving. It is significant that one of the art forms most open to interpretation, that is, most open to experiencing the echo of a great human passion, is opera. By the conventions of operatic form and style, by the arias and melodies, by the power of music, passion is fully expressed. But we speak here of an affective movement that takes on an extreme modality. Thus, we must invoke another classification.

		Concupiscible (libido)	*Irascible* (aggressivité)
Relation to sensible good	In itself Absent Absent and difficult to obtain Absent and impossible to obtain	Love Desire Pleasure	 Hope Despair
Relation to sensible evil	In itself Absent Absent but avoidable Absent but inevitable Present and surmountable Present and insurmountable	Hate Aversion Sorrow	 Courage Fear Anger

18

Sentiments, Emotions, Passions

O N THE TOPIC OF THE AFFECTIVE movements, called, as a group, "passions" by the ancients, modern psychologists have made distinctions of great value. They propose another classification, according to the modalities that these affective movements take on in the concrete life of a subject, the being that performs acts. Joy, sorrow, courage, fear can present themselves either as *sentiments,* or as *emotions,* or, finally, as "passions," in a different sense of the word. These distinctions will afford us more complete entry into the dark domain of the affectivity.

In order to facilitate an understanding of this classification, let us list its criteria. An affective moment (1) is underpinned by knowledge of the object; (2) has a physiological accompaniment; (3) governs a conduct with regard to a situation. In terms of the manner in which these three constitutive elements are experienced, we find ourselves in the presence of a sentiment, or an emotion, or a passion.

Sentiment

We have a sentiment when the affective movement is underpinned by a balanced knowledge of its object. The affectivity bestows upon perception an enhanced capacity of attention, a facilitated penetration. Sentiment favors knowledge. Sentiment renders its subject, the soul, "clear-eyed." Affectivity is saved, as it were, by thought. Its physiological echo is peaceful. It is comparable to the current of a tranquil river. Furthermore, deep within its subject, it lends balance, self-possession, self-control. The case is the same for external behavior: a sentiment adapts the activity of its subject to the changing circumstances of things, and to the fluctuations of sensibility. In a word, sentiment is rightness of soul and affective maturity.

Emotion

The balance always bestowed by sentiment is threatened by those brief crises of the affection called the emotions. Emotion is an intense affective movement whose effect is to disturb the mental functions. To be moved is to lose control of one's mind. "Emotion" comes from the Latin, *ex-movere,* which can be translated "leave oneself," or "be out of oneself." In emotion, the mind is misled, the judgment paralyzed. In addition, emotion is accompanied by a sharp breach in the bodily equilibrium: circulatory and muscular disturbances. Racine describes perfectly the interior agitation of Phaedra at the sight of Hippolytus, the object of her insane love:

> I saw him, I flushed, I grew pale at his sight,
> A turmoil emerged in my desperate soul:
> Mine eyes saw no longer, nor could I speak,
> I felt all my body benumbed yet aflame.

Finally, emotion impairs behavior. It impels the subject, the "doer," to act in a way contrary to the demands of the situation. It nails one's feet to the floor when one ought to flee. One faints dead away when one ought to be mobilizing all of one's energies. The vocabulary employed to translate it reveals this "mental earthquake": now the language is no longer of fear, but of dread, horror, panic, terror.

Passion (New Meaning)

Now we speak of passion in its new acceptation. While emotion is a sudden, brief crisis of affectivity, passion is a crisis that takes hold of its subject, the impassioned one, and lasts. A crisis of the sentiment, passion acts upon the mental functions, first by narrowing the field of one's awareness. The impassioned person is obsessed and becomes incapable of really opening to the world of others. Fixed on a single object, his or her mind loses the mobility that characterizes a free consciousness. We may recall Molière's Miser, who, everywhere and in every circumstance, is incapable of ever speaking of anything except his money. Passion jumbles the sentiments, draining them of all psychic energy of the soul for its profit. It dominates, subjugates, and finally kills affectivity. The subject of passion cannot adapt to the spectrum of her or his manifold duties, and to the decencies of life in society. As we see, taken in this sense passion is a psychological evil, although it can also become, in certain cases, the rich soil for the growth of a great artistic work.

19

The Affective Keys

*The human condition: inconstancy, ennui,
inner turmoil.*

—Pascal

IN MODERN PHILOSOPHY, certain sentiments have become the object of a new analysis. The manner in which they spread throughout the depths of the soul has earned them the name of "affective keys."

An affective key is a fundamental state securing the coloration of a person's entire life. The term "key" indicates that we are dealing with an impregnation of the whole soul by a particular sentiment: gladness, sorrow, anxiety, anguish. But in this particular case it is not a matter of an ordinary sentiment. And first of all, the affective key does not relate to a determined, precise object. It fails to refer to an external thing that one could name. For example, if we ask the subject why she is anguished, she will respond, "For no reason." German philosopher Martin Heidegger, who bases his teaching on the key of anguish, writes: "There is nothing determinate in the world over which the human being suffers anguish."[6]

But to say that the affective key has no precise object does not mean that it does not have an object. Its object is *the world as a whole*. It is to the totality of that which exists, to the totality of things, that the affective key relates. Only, this relation is experienced in such a way that knower and known are blended into one another in a mutual impregnation. "The affective key," continues Heidegger, "comes *neither from without nor from within*, but wells up as a mode of being-in-the-world [that originates precisely] from [being-in-the-world.] The affective key plunges to the stratum where subject and object form a primordial unity in the soul."[7]

There is more. The philosophers of existence attribute to affectivity as thus analyzed the power to reveal the mystery of being. Anguish, for example, is felt in the face of "nothing." But thanks to "nothingness," which advances toward me, then, the strangeness of the world appears to me. When every purchase and fulcrum are denied me, then and only then am I in a condition to "see" existence as a mystery, a question. In the world of ordinary sentiments, "existence" is always a fact that goes without saying. When, on the contrary, the totality of things withdraws into indifference, when everything that has attached me to precise things is undone, then alone are the basic questions posed to me.

These reflections are intended to afford a glimpse of how, with the existentialist philosophers, the affectivity of the human soul touches the very foundations of existence. Until now, metaphysics has been a domain where one could enter only by the pathways of logic, and by concepts. The experience of anguish, of ennui, of nausea, of anxiety, on the contrary, is regarded by these philosophers as the only authentic path truly leading to the very heart of existence and its mystery. The interest of these analyses is undeniable. Still, we have to say that such meditations on these forms of affectivity do not progress beyond the area of psychology. Psychology has been stretched until it "mimics metaphysics."[8]

Conclusion of Part 3

O UR PART 3 HAS TESTIFIED to another aspect of the life of the human soul. Knowledge is not the sole finality of the body that it builds and composes, fashioning it of such finely wrought organs. After all, the living being must appropriate things for its subsistence—first for its growth, then for its maintenance. It must also avoid the forces that can diminish it and cause it to die. These two duties are performed on behalf of the soul thanks to the affective powers: sentiments, emotions, passions. These psychic movements stimulate the appearance of conduits that the soul invents in order to react to the most varied and unforeseeable situations. What is remarkable in this area is that sentiments, emotions, and passions regulate no behaviors without somehow sculpting the forms of the appetite in the matter of the body.

It will be worthwhile to cite the manner in which the soul relates to the play of these bodily modifications. St. Thomas Aquinas has shown that the soul operates according to an analogy between the psychic order and the physical order (*Summa Theologiae* I-II, q. 44, a. 1). It creates relations of similarity between these two orders. Let us take *fear*, for example. On the psychic level, fear consists in a movement of with-

63

drawal of the appetite. Fear proceeds from the fact that the imagination represents the threat of evil. But it is a difficult evil to repel. The reason for this is that the subject of this feeling, the person in whom this feeling occurs, lacks strength. And the more pronounced this lack of force is, the more the field of his or her action shrinks. Now, this is what the soul represents to the body itself by muscular retraction and the loss of vitality. Here is the image of what is happening in the soul, projected upon the body. Interpreted in this way, these facts afford a glimpse of how the human soul models its body to its likeness.

Is it not owing to a heightened consciousness of this power that the art of the dance was born? Paul Valéry, at any rate, ascribes to this art the clear "revelation to our souls of what our bodies accomplish obscurely."[9] Thus, the sensible affective life and its transfer to the organs have this as their end: to "make souls imagine by means of bodies."[10]

It occurs in certain cases that the affective life of the human soul is no longer shared by the body. The soul somehow escapes. Sometimes it even goes so far as to oppose the body. And so we have not yet said everything about the affective life of the soul. Now we must examine the acts in which the affective life of the human being is "full of spirit," of mind. These are her free acts.

Part 4

Human Beings: Their Freedom and Subjectivity

The great mystery of personal freedom is that even God pauses before it.

—St. Edith Stein

20

Birth of the Will

*Good must be shown to us in order that
we may be able to yield to the inclination
that bears us toward it.*

—Louis Lavelle

W ITH THE WILL, WE CROSS a new threshold of human
affectivity. Here we must cite Aristotle's declaration in
his treatise *On the Soul*. "The will is born in human reason"
(3.432b.5). Let us not surrender this insight. What it says is
precious: that the intellect and will are closely connected faculties. Even though they operate in two different spheres—
knowing and appetite—they are nevertheless interdependent,
and, as it were, married to each other. As we shall see later,
there is an act, the free act, that is the fruit of their mutual
involvement. And this act, for certain thinkers, defines the
human being: *the human being is freedom.*

Aristotle is correct, then. The will is born at the very heart
of the intellect. How is this birth to be explained? Everything
in the human being begins with the senses. We have strongly
emphasized this apropos of the activity of the intellect. We
form no idea without reference to the senses. The same must
be said regarding the spiritual appetite, the will. Before making an act of the will—or, better, in order to be able to make
it—the human being has had to experience innumerable sensible affections. The moment these movements of the sensible

appetite act, we must not believe that the intellect is not involved with them. Everything having to do with the senses is experienced by the intellect, as well, but in its own way. Now, its own way of reacting to the things that occur in the sphere of the senses is to make itself "ideas" of them. And so, while the senses are busy seeing colors and smelling the scent of individual roses, an idea is formed in the intellect in an abstract and universal representation.

We must say the same thing apropos of our experiences of affectivity. While the sensible appetite is experiencing pleasure over a particular good, the intellect forms within itself the idea of good. What is represented in this idea of good is no longer such and such a particularized, concrete good. It is the totality of "Good." A Good lacking in nothing! In order to render their reference to this Good more expressive, speakers of French take the adjective *bon,* "good," and build it into *bonheur,* "happiness." St. Augustine himself implies the connection when he asks, "Is not that to which all aspire, and which no one disdains, happiness?" (*Confessions* 10.20). Pascal, too, uses the word *bonheur,* "happiness," to evoke its transcendence with respect to all particular goods. "All persons seek to be happy— there are no exceptions. Regardless of the different means they employ, they all strain toward this goal. . . . The will never takes the least step but toward this object. This is the motive of all actions of all persons, including those about to hang themselves" (*Pensées,* Brunschwig, no. 425).

St. Augustine, then, poses the question "Where has happiness ever been seen, so as to be loved? Certainly it is within us. But how? I know not" (*Confessions* 10.20). St. Thomas Aquinas has explained how happiness is indeed within us. First he explains that it is the intellect that forms the idea of "good," from a starting point in the experience of sensible goods. Then he states that the appetite tends toward the good. But he advises caution here. The appetite is a realistic faculty. We have seen this when we spoke of love. What love tends to is not an "idea" but the reality that the idea presents to it. Seeking happiness, the appetite tends toward a reality in which, existentially, the totality of "Good" is to be found, a Good lacking in nothing. Then what is born in the heart of the intellect is a new appetite. And this appetite awakens with all the more power when the Good that it desires is the greatest of Goods!

21

Freedom at the Heart of the Will

Affectivity draws me out of myself when it plunges me to the depths of myself.
—Louis Lavelle

IT IS ON ACCOUNT OF THE INTELLECT that the will develops in the human soul. The will springs up as a new appetite. This appetite is spiritual. The idea of the "good" is a representation that forms in the mind, not in the senses. The first act of the will is to appeal to the intellect that it go in quest of this good. What reality, what concrete thing, could crown its infinite desire? After all, an appetite is not satisfied with an idea, and thus the will is not satisfied with the idea of happiness. It wants this happiness in flesh and blood!

By reason of the origin of the will in the intellect, the two faculties embrace in a common activity. The first fruit of their cooperation is the production of an absolutely first truth. It is a first principle in the order of activity. It is formulated thus: *Happiness is what I want.* This judgment, it is clear, orders or points the one who pronounces it to action. But there also opens before him an abyss, a chasm. The sensible appetites, for their part, are borne to delimited, finite, singular goods— to nutrition, for example, or to reproduction. But where are the boundaries of the universal Good? And what limits enclose happiness? Thus it is in the desire of an infinite amplitude that the root of freedom resides. If the will has for its object a Good to which nothing is lacking in the line of good, and tends to it necessarily, then it cannot tend necessarily to a finite, limited, particular good. Absence of inner necessity is called freedom: free choice.

Why do we use, just as accurately, the word "liberty" for freedom or free choice? Etymology will tell us. "Liberty" comes from the Latin *librare,* which means "weigh." Free choice, then, is a judgment that consists in weighing the goods that are presented to the will. And the measure by which we weigh these goods is the Good, the universal essence of Good. We have just observed that the very first judgment of the voluntary appetite united to the intellect is formulated: "Happiness," or "the Good is what I want." And this absolute Good is henceforth the scales on which the will is to weigh every possible good it ever confronts. Every thing presented to the "willing" will be weighed against the weight of the Good, the weight of happiness. Such an appetite does not perform its movement toward its object *impulsively.* It will de*libera*te. It will weigh the goods. Aristotle calls the will the "deliberative" faculty (*On the Soul* 3.433b.4).

The question we must now ask ourselves is this: Is it possible to say *how* this "weighing" of goods offered to the will takes place? How does the will fix its choice?

As we have said, intellect and will are "married" to each other, as it were. Let us imagine the following conversation between these two faculties. The will asks the intellect, which has generated it with the idea of the good, "Show me where, in what concrete thing, I can find this Good to which nothing is lacking." But in each finite, particular good that it encounters, the intellect cannot fail to see that its pursuit and possession necessarily entail the privation of other goods. For instance, to devote one's life to study is certainly a desirable thing. But I cannot fail to see that this entails the renunciation of other goods. And the case is the same for everything—even for God, inasmuch as I have not had the vision of God! Accordingly, the intellect can only respond to the will's request by saying, "Of everything I weigh against the weight of the Good, I can only say: 'This is good, but . . . it is not yet the Good.'" The intellect is in equilibrium. It cannot escape this oscillation. From every search it returns with the same response: "This is good, but . . . ."

With its appetite for happiness, the will refuses to accept this "indetermination" on the part of the intellect. The intellect cannot arrive at a judgment that presents it with the Good, with happiness itself. The will itself must intervene. It is the will itself that will now weigh all of the weight of the Good, of happiness itself, against a particular thing. It determines the intelligence to say, for example, "a life devoted to study is what is good for me." In itself "determining" the intellect to this kind of judgment, the will is self-determining. Now, what is freedom but the self-determination of the will?

22

The Common Sense Finds the Perfect Formula

The human being is defined only by the infinite.
—Dom Jean-Baptiste Porion

THE CONCLUSION OF THE ANALYSIS of the preceding chapter, admittedly rather technical, is surprisingly confirmed by the insight of common sense (in the ordinary usage of the word this time). We occasionally hear someone say, "She staked all her happiness on . . . ." Popular language says this of someone who has chosen a particular kind of life, or who is passionately attached even to a futile thing. This reflection contains a most profound insight into the power of freedom. And Yves Simon is altogether correct when he writes, apropos of this manner of speaking: "No philosopher would be able to find a more accurate formula. To stake one's happiness on a particular good is to give this particular good the quantity of complementary goodness of which it has need in order to become desirable absolutely."[1] It is marvelous to see the concurrence, in such a delicate question, of the immediate data of awareness with the technical subtleties of philosophy!

However, one point remains unexplained. How does it happen that the human being does not see that the good he has chosen will always be, despite everything, a particular, limited, finite realization of the Good? How does it happen that there is an attraction here capable of outweighing everything else? Must we not conclude that I can place my happiness in what I wish? This question must be answered in the affirmative. And we must add, with Yves Simon: "I can place my happiness where I wish because I wish to be happy."[2]

To be free means for the human soul to enjoy the privilege of choosing its ends. It can choose its ends because it is in its nature to tend to an end that is beyond the finite. A contemplative who values his anonymity has written:

> Freedom is conceivable only as the privilege of a transcendent certitude: the human being can give himself his means and his ends, because his End is beyond doubt, beyond the finite. If he is a dancer and juggler among beings—still he stands and moves on the hardest soil. It is by relying on a deeper need than the "I," more assured than its existence, that he can lift, raise, and send flying, everything, including himself.

Could we find a better translation of the sentiment that seizes the human soul when it realizes that it has the privilege of being free? Then this soul experiences the fact that nothing, absolutely nothing to be found here below, is capable of determining it. Now it has the experience that it is spirit. How will it not be drunk with its lightness, its sheer buoyancy! In his "Bateau ivre" ("Drunken Boat"), Rimbaud sings: "Crease, keel, the waves! I must down to the sea!"

23

Freedom and Subjectivity

Liberty and consciousness are but one.
—Louis Lavelle

THANKS TO HER FREE ACTS, the human being attains subjectivity. This may be the most precious effect of freedom of choice. By "subjectivity," we mean that the human being doubly becomes the subject of her actions.

Let us return to our years in grade school, when we were taught to diagram sentences. "This person is a traveler," the teacher would write on the board. Then we would diagram that sentence in a way that would indicate "person" as the *subject* and "is a traveler" as the predicate, with "is" as the verb and "traveler" as the predicate noun. The verb "is" ties the predicate noun to the subject. This sort of analysis of the sentence taken here as an example reveals that the act of traveling *belongs* to "this person." And that is equivalent to saying that he or she is the cause of the traveling. It means that, in the act of exercising this activity, he or she enjoys a certain autonomy, a certain independence. Grammar implies a whole philosophy.

Now, we have to say that the subject who "places," who "posits," a free act posits it in all independence. As we have seen, it is an act that has been weighed. It has not been posited necessarily. The subject of the act has committed himself to it

by personally constituting the reasons he himself has for positing it. Not only does this act belong to him now, but he knows
that it belongs to him. This is *subjectivity.*

The better to penetrate this privilege, let us compare the
free act of a human being with the act of a plant or animal.
This rose in my garden develops, nourishes itself, and is inter-
nally organized. These acts belong to it. But it does not choose
to perform these acts. They are imposed upon it by nature, as
is, for that matter, its manner of performing them. Its program of life is drawn up in advance. Its acts do not belong to
it completely. Now let us watch a swallow as it darts across the
sky, in search of nourishment. Most of the acts it posits are
commanded it by its nature. But its flight, for example, is not
drawn up in advance. It itself invents by its perceptions and
interiorizes the ceaselessly changing directions of this flight.
Here its acts belong to it. It has more independence in its
activity. Compared to a plant, an animal enjoys a far greater
independence.

To be sure, the human being also has an end imposed upon
her: *the* end, the supreme goal of all. She tends necessarily
toward the Good, toward happiness simple and infinite. But
precisely, the nature of *the* end is so transcendent to all concrete, particular ends that none of these is imposed on her.
While she does not decide *the* end as her end, she decides all
the other ends. She gives herself the guise she wishes: she will
be a physician, a farmer, a nun, an artist, and so on. Clearly, to
be able to create her ends brings the human being to a *new
independence* in the line of activity. In a new sense, she is the
subject of these activities.

Furthermore, human beings know themselves as the *subject*
of their activities. As we have observed: the free act is the fruit
of the conjoined operation of the intellect and will. "The will
is in the intellect," said Aristotle. This being the case, if a free

act is formed in them, it is therefore in the intelligence, and therefore necessarily known (St. Thomas Aquinas, *IP*, q. 87, a. 1). And so, in the free act, the subject who will perform it knows himself as subject of this act. And this is to acquire subjectivity.

Louis Lavelle has made this profound observation:

> Freedom and consciousness are but one. How, indeed, could a person be free, and deprived of consciousness? And of what could one have consciousness other than the being that one gives oneself, not in separating oneself from the world, but in turning to the world an initiative that is proper to us?[3]

In defining freedom as having consciousness of the being that one gives oneself, Lavelle hits upon a formula that reveals not only the metaphysical import of freedom but, thereby, as well, the drama into which a person is plunged.

24

The Aspiration to Surpass the Human

If there were gods, how could I endure not being God?
—Friedrich Nietzsche

THE FREE ACT AWAKENS subjectivity in a person—a new independence among the beings of nature. To be able to decide one's own end is to choose one's face. It is to be no longer constrained, in order to realize oneself, to follow a route already traced out. It can happen that a person experiences the privilege of being ruler of his or her acts to the point of inebriation.

Independence in the domain of action is a transcendental "perfection," or concrete attribute. "Transcendental" means that the object so described is not confined to any category, as here with the perfection known as independence. We see independence appearing even in the plant, which exercises, of itself, the operations by which it is constituted. Independence increases with the animal, which, by its own perceptions, invents the pathways of its activities. With the human being, it asserts itself even more, since, instead of receiving the ends of his actions from a nature, he gives them to himself.

A transcendental perfection, by definition (*trans* + *ascendere*, to "ascend beyond") cannot halt in a category in its ascent. It demands of itself an absolute realization. And this is verified precisely in the case of the human being. In this line of independence, she aspires to take leave of the limits nevertheless encountered by independence in its creaturely condition. The human being suffers from a divine illness!

We need only think of modern atheism. Feuerbach, for example, invites the human being to recover to her own account the divine essence that, from weakness, she has projected upon another Being outside herself. Nietzsche used to say, "The human being must be surpassed."[4] This aspiration to surpass the human to the point of self-divinization finds its most impassioned expression in Kirillov, a personage in Dostoyevsky's novel *The Possessed:* "Three years I have sought the attribute of my divinity, and I have found it. It is my will. It is everything by which I can show, to its capital point, my insubordination, and my terrible freedom."[5]

Human beings know, then, in the depths of their will, an aspiration to depend henceforward on nothing but themselves. Kirillov's torment lurks in the hidden caverns of every free creature. Nowhere as much as in the most frenzied pages of modern atheists can we find the echo of the suggestion of the serpent of creation: "You shall be as God."

Yes, there, in the depths of human creativity, is where the universe of morality and immorality finds its origin.

A person may consent to this excess, this seeking to-be-like God. Then he constitutes himself the center of all, to the point of contempt for God and a denial of the rights of his Creator. Or else a person may accept the fact that he did not create himself, so that it is God who is absolute subjectivity. Then he consents to refer all things to God, including his very being.

The will necessarily plunges the human being into a metaphysical drama. But by that very fact, it reveals to him his greatness!

Conclusion of Part 4

SURELY THE FREEDOM of the human soul is a privilege. It is the power by which the human soul holds all things in suspense. This power is fashioned on a judgment born in us with the first act of intelligence. One can formulate this judgment in the following terms: "What I want is happiness—a Good without limit, a Good that satisfies all of my appetites." We do not express this judgment in an explicit way. Most of the time, we carry it within ourselves unformulated. We carry it in our unconscious, in the source of our mind. "There is a whole life, both intuitive and unexpressed, that precedes rational explanations."[6]

And so we descend amidst the things of this world in an equilibrium, in a balance whose measure is the infinite Good. It is against this measure of weight that all things are weighed. It has been said:

> The intellect is mobile, and mobilizes things, because it is balanced on a divine, inner, intangible point. For the intellect as for a scales, freedom is justice. The ruling independence of the judgment, which is the root of that of the will-act, requires a yardstick, an act, a fixed, secret point making it possible to measure, weigh, and set in rotation all the rest. It is the sovereign simplicity of the anonymous criterion that guarantees our enfranchisement and poise with regard to every object.

The power of human freedom is akin to that of God. And so freedom hurls the human being into the drama of a choice in which these two freedoms necessarily come in conflict, or else the human being's freedom acquiesces in its free submission to that of God, thereby finding its salvation! The poet of the psalm entitled "Munificence of the Creator" cries out:

> You have made the human being little less than a god!
> With glory and splendor have you crowned him.
> You have set him over the work of your hands;
> you have put all things under his feet. (Psalm 8:6–7)

Part 5

Human Beings:
Soul and Spirit

It is unreasonable to admit that the intellect is intermixed with the body.

—Aristotle

25

The Soul Is the Substance of the Human Being

The person is "hatched" from the soul, which forms the center of its being.

—St. Edith Stein

FROM THE VERY BEGINNING of these pages, we have spoken of the human soul, architect of its body, source of its faculties of knowledge and affectivity. The soul infuses these faculties in organs to use as instruments, as tools. Not that our method will be altogether immune to objection. One criticism, in particular, will be that we "beg the question." To begin by speaking of the soul—is this not to assume without proof what precisely should first be proved? Many philosophers think that the most that can be done in psychology is to analyze functions of the human being. They practice what has been called a "psychology without a soul"!

It is certainly true that we do not see the soul. But we discern it. We glimpse it behind the curtain of its operations. It is true that, in order really to reach it, the intellect must build itself a bridge of light, that is, of reasoning. This is what we shall now undertake.

Let us return, then, to those who purely and simply deny the existence of the soul. One may not speak—their argument runs—of that of which there is no perception, external or internal. But the soul is not visible to the eyes, nor palpable to the touch, nor is it possible to form an image of it, since an image can be formed only of what one has previously seen, touched, heard. There is no soul, there are only phenomena. Thus, we must step onto the terrain where phenomenalists and substantialists collide.

Phenomenalism is the doctrine that reduces all bodies, and so'the human being, as well, to phenomena. Let us explain the term "phenomenon." It comes from the Greek. Its root is *pha-*, which is also the root of *phōs*. Now, *phōs* means "light" (cf. "phosphorescent"). The phenomenon, then, is what "comes to light" in a thing—a flower, an animal, a human being. But that which in the human being comes to the light of consciousness are his operations, known either by perception or by introspection. In a human being, say the phenomenalists, one finds nothing but its manifestations of consciousness. For example, consider the celebrated formula of Jean-Paul Sartre: "Being is nothing but the closely joined series of its manifestations."[1] With one stroke of the pen, Sartre annihilates substance. It no longer enjoys "citizenship," as he puts it.[2] With the same stroke the soul is gone as well. Along with substance, the soul is an illusion left over from a world dead and gone.[3]

We take cognizance of these peremptory pronouncements, but in order to criticize them in our own turn. Let us make two observations.

To say with Sartre, "Being is nothing but the closely joined series of its manifestations" is to be guilty of a remarkable piece of question-begging. In the very sentence by which he ostracizes substance, he surreptitiously reintroduces it. After all, to say, "Being is nothing but the closely joined series of its manifestations" is to say that phenomena are joined by themselves. This means that what is joined is what joins. And this is a contradiction! It is saying that the manifold is the cause of the one. And that is an absurdity!

We must make a second comment. In *Being and Nothingness,* where he professes a total phenomenalism, Sartre explains *why* he eliminates substance and therefore soul. Substance, according to Sartre, would be a ready-made reality positioned *under* operations, hidden *behind* operations, behind the manifestations of the human being. But to present substance in this way is to caricature it in order to be able to deny it! The notion of substance as Aristotle establishes it is entirely different. We find a perfect explanation in Jacques Maritain:

> It is the first ontological root of each thing in its permanent actuality, in its essential unity, in its irreducible reality, in its specific, individual originality. Far from being empty, far from being inert, it is the source of all faculties, all operations, all activity, and the subject's causality.[4]

Admittedly, the soul is to be distinguished from its faculties and operations. But because it is one and the same through time, and because from it all of the faculties emanate, therefore it is the soul that permits the reference of a series of multiple, changing operations to one and the same subject. It is the link. It is the soul, one and identical, which legitimates it that the series of manifestations of which the history of a human being is woven becomes perfectly unified, perfectly identifiable. Otherwise their attribution to one and the same subject, to one and the same "I," would have no foundation. It would be, as it were, suspended in the void!

To conclude: Each human individual is a substance thanks to the soul. This is because the soul is substance. Now that we have explained its existence, it is possible to delve into it to tell its mystery, especially its state as spirit.

26

The Human Soul Is Also Spirit

It is in its inmost self, in its essence or in its depths, that the soul is actually at home.
—St. Edith Stein

THE READER IS AWARE THAT, in these pages, especially in parts 1 and 2, we have endeavored to demonstrate how intimate to the human being is the union of body and soul. The soul, Aristotle said, does the work of an engineer, adjusting organs to their functions. It also does the work of an architect, arranging the organs in a whole, which whole is its body. It is correct to call the soul the *form of the body.* Only, the word "form" is not to be understood in the sense of outer shape. It means inner, dynamic, formative "principle" (concrete basis), the molder of matter. Aristotle defines the soul as "the form of a natural body having life in potency" (*On the Soul* 2.2.412a. 20). Or again, the "first act of an organized natural body" (2.2.412b.5).

We must now add that the soul is more than a "form that gives life to the body, more than the internal of an external," to speak with St. Edith Stein.[5]

When we were considering the soul, which uses the organs that it has itself built for its life of knowledge and affectivity, we skipped over the sensible world in each of these spheres. We have seen the soul seek still other objects than those presented to it by the senses. We have seen it seek *being* when it knows, something before which the external and internal senses are blind. The human soul seeks to know more and asks, "What is it?" The senses cannot answer this question. We have likewise seen, in the affective sphere, how the soul seeks the Good, the universal essence of Good. The senses cannot answer this question. They bring the soul only limited, finite goods.

Aristotle observed the same thing. There is "an operation that seems proper to the soul. It is the act of thinking" (*On the Soul* 1.1.403a.11–12). We can add: ". . . And the act of willing the Good." For Aristotle, then, there are acts in the human being in which the soul alone acts. "The body does not share in it" (Aristotle, *On the Generation of Animals* 2.3.736b.29). In such acts, the soul emerges from its act of being the form of the body and enters into the condition of spirit.

Let us repeat: when the soul performs certain acts—thinking and willing—and the external and internal senses cannot have been the suppliers of these objects, the human soul acts as a spirit. By this we mean that it is no longer dependent on the body. But this actually happens in every act of thought and free will. Aristotle remarked in astonishment: "The intellect acually seems to [act] in us as possessing a substantial existence, and not to be subject to corruption" (*On the Soul* 1.4. 408b.18). Let us keep this sentence in mind. It is upon the independence of the human soul vis-à-vis matter—therefore on its immateriality, as it will later be called—that Aristotle founds its immortality.

We see how difficult it is to speak of "the human being's being" with precision. Granted, the human soul is the *form* of its body, as the soul of a periwinkle is the form of its body.

Still, the soul of a flower or of an animal does not possess existence for itself. These souls—of vegetables or animals—cannot subsist alone, without their bodies. And the reason for this is that such souls perform all of their operations in dependence on their bodies. The human soul, by contrast, being independent of the body in certain of its acts, can exist without its body. And yet there are not two substances in the human being. It is of the *very nature* of the human soul to *inform,* as philosophers say, give form to, a body. After all, it is the senses, bound to the bodily organs, that bring to the soul objects upon which the intellect acts by knowing them, and this is the soul's very first act upon these objects.

27

Life of the Soul as Spirit

The human soul breathes above time.
—Jacques Maritain

IN THIS CHAPTER we shall examine the soul leading its life of spirit. We shall do so by observing the work it performs in the act of abstraction.

We have insisted a great deal on sensible knowledge in the life of the soul. Now we must insist no less on another psychological fact. We shall now consider the fact that the soul's life of sensible knowledge and sensible affectivity is but a stepping-stone to its life as spirit. The soul does not stop at the sphere of the sensible. That is not its goal, the end that it seeks. On the contrary, it is in going beyond that sphere for the sake of being able to think, it is for the sake of willing with free will, going beyond the senses, that the soul exercises its complex sensible life, external and internal.

We human beings perceive ourselves, imagine ourselves, remember ourselves, but we also go beyond these acts. We can demonstrate this by analyzing the process of *abstraction*. This is the word we use to define the work performed by the intellect in the genesis of its ideas, its concepts. But let us pay particular attention to the end that it seeks in this work.

Everything in our psychic life begins with sensations. These are numberless, teeming. Still, they are spontaneously "synthesized," united, by the inner faculty called the "common sense." This sense joins together in a single object all of the various data that come from things. This yellow color, this acidic taste, this textured surface, this scent—all of this is joined together in such a way that I can give this fruit its name: the name "lemon." The object thus unified passes into the imagination, which retains only a sketch of it as a sensible object. But in this internal sensible structure, an intelligible is present. "It is in sensible forms that intelligibles exist" (*On the Soul* 3.8. 432a.4–5). Then, to borrow one of Aristotle's images once more, the intellect seizes it, like a hand, *abstracts* it, draws it to itself, into itself, and finally, expresses it as the product of this "simple apprehension"—this "simple prehension" or grasping—giving it its name, the name "lemon."

The soul conducts this process of abstraction under pressure of the intellect. It sets afoot all of its faculties of sensible knowing in order to permit the intellect to "draw," out of the complex sensible datum, progressively structured, the essence of things. This work of abstraction is not an end for the soul. It does not stop there. But it must move along the route of this step. It stops its work when, in having penetrated the essence of things to its depths, it "reads" that essence, thanks to the production of the *idea* in which it sees that essence. ("Intellect" is from the Latin "*intus legere,*" to "read inwardly." "Idea" is from the Greek *eidein,* to "see.")

In order to "see" essences, then, the intellect has had to "abstract" them (from the Latin *abs-tractum,* "drawn out"). It has had to extract them from matter. But then the senses continue to be blind, as it were, with regard to such objects. The latter are known only by the intellect. In this act on the part of the intelligence, the senses no longer have any part. Thus the soul is no longer acting as the form of its body. That is why it is said to be leading a life of spirit. Aristotle, author of the doctrine of "abstraction" sketched here, concluded that the intellect in the human soul is a very different faculty, or part, from the others. And he added, "Only the intellect can be separated from the body" (*On the Soul* 2.2.413b26). It is in this precise sense that the soul must be called *spirit*. In its intellective acts, the soul is justly said to "breathe above time." We likewise see how close Aristotle came to a proof of the immortality of the soul. True, he did not explicitly articulate this proof. But he has done more. He has indicated what needs to be examined in order to establish such a proof. In his thought, he had the vivid intuition of the principle that lies at its foundation. It is Aristotle who has said of the intelligence that it is "something divine, and incapable of being acted upon" (*On the Soul* 1.4.408b.29).

28

Life of the Soul as Spirit (Continuation)

An old person who could find an eye of good quality would see just as clearly as a young person.
—Aristotle

THE LIFE OF THE SOUL as spirit begins with the phase of abstraction set forth in the preceding chapter. Abstraction is not only the very first work of the soul as spirit. It actually forms the underpinning of all of the human being's spiritual activities. We should like to examine, here, two activities of the soul in which the independence of the soul with respect to matter clearly appears. We shall speak first of the quest for definitions, and then, in the next chapter, of artistic creativity.

Quest for Definitions

Aristotle said that Socrates' greatest merit was to have created the method of definition. By way of example, we should have to select one or other of Plato's Socratic dialogues in which the author portrays Socrates as ever in pursuit of definitions. His dialectical method consisted in gathering together only the common elements of a group of things, while excluding all individual elements. The definition of the human being—"rational animal"—permits within itself neither height, nor weight, nor color, nor age, nor language—nothing that belongs to the individual person as individual. It is obvious, then, that, when we utter a definition, our intellect is presenting nothing sensible, nothing material. If we doubt this, we need only open a dictionary and read the definitions of a few nouns. The nouns will all be given abstractly, and the definitions that accompany them will also be abstract. Here is proof that, in order to define them, the human soul snatches the essences of the world from nature and "detemporalizes" them, "despatializes" them.

Charles Journet writes:

I look at the things around me. When I speak of them, if I wish to communicate with you I am obliged, for you to grasp my thought, to snatch them from their milieu. I communicate to them their essence. And you, in your turn, receive this communication as an animal could not receive it—you receive it as despatialized and detemporalized. One who performs the action of snatching a reality from its spatio-temporal milieu, and one who hears [the former], have this same power—the power to establish a language above space and time.[6]

This is how you can show the independence of the human soul vis-à-vis time and space. The mode according to which essences are above time indicates the mode according to which the human soul is above time.

Extracting a further conclusion, Aristotle does not fear to assert that spirit, as such, does not age, does not grow old! When one is nearly eighty years old, one cannot transcribe the following text without humor and delight.

An old person who could find an eye of good quality would see just as clearly as a young person. In other words, old age is due *not to any affection of the soul,* but to an affection of the subject [the body] in which [the soul] resides, just as occurs in intoxication or illness. The exercise of thought and knowing, then, declines when *another organ,* an internal one is destroyed, but in itself the intellect is incapable of suffering decline. (*On the Soul,* 1.4.408b.20–25)

Let us inscribe it on the fleshy tablets of our hearts! Living a life of spirit, the soul does not age. Therefore it must be immortal.

29

Life of the Soul as Spirit (Conclusion)

The one unwilling to die.

—*Epic of Gilgamesh*

THE WORK OF DEFINITION, then, implies an extraction of essences from their spatio-temporal framework. There is yet another activity in which the independence of the human soul with regard to matter is attested just as forcefully:

Artistic Activity

In order the better to enter into the mystery of artistic creation, let us entertain this preliminary reflection. The things of nature can be called God's works of art. In each thing, in this daisy, in this swallow, there is an essence. But what is an essence? An essence is a creative idea that God has instilled in matter in order that it accomplish a specific program of life there. This daisy grows in conformity with the idea of daisy. St. Thomas Aquinas liked to say that the nature of things is a divine art residing in things (*Contra Gentiles* 3.3). Most of the time this aspect of things vanishes under the veil of their potential as "utensils." We regard them from the angle of their utility for ourselves. But let the veil suddenly rend, and let them appear for themselves, in the splendor of their first vocation—then the soul is deliciously wounded. This is the privilege of the artist.

When, suddenly, a thing of nature—a tree, a bird, the humblest thing lets a ray of this divine light in it escape, then subjectivity awakes to itself and is revealed to itself. Baudelaire, evoking the mystery of poetic knowledge, writes: "Things think in me; I think myself in them." Now there is born in the soul the irrepressible need to carry this thing away with us, as one removes a primrose, with the earth around its roots, because one is unwilling to see it perish!

But the work of art is not only a hieroglyph for the artist of his or her soul; it is also, according to Malraux's formulation, "the legal tender of the Absolute."[7] Thus, there would be, at the origin of the work of art, a more radical aspiration than the thrust to express a subjectivity. There would be a need to save things from the decay of time, from the grasp of the death that destroys all. There would be, in the work of the artist, the will to pull a thing of the world from contingency and transport it into the world of pure space.

From this viewpoint, Malraux has classified all of the great works of art, paintings and sculptures, in three categories, under three heads: the *supernatural,* the *unreal,* and the *atemporal.* Just in themselves, these three titles speak of the existence of another world!

In artistic creation, the independence of spirit is no longer asserted in removing matter, as if neglecting it. Rather, the artist struggles with it, remaining in it. In order to transport a form of being to where it can be saved from death, in the supernatural or unreal or atemporal, the artist no longer works as does the philosopher. It is into the matter of the marble, or of the colors, that she inserts the spiritual that she has seen fleetingly shimmer in things. And she causes the spiritual to appear by procedures that may have changed over the centuries. Hence the three successive steps covered by Malraux's division. Geometrization of bodies, deformation of proportions, abstraction of the accidental, exaltation of colors—such, among others, are the procedures thanks to which the sculptor and the painter strive to extract things from time, to pluck them from death, to introduce them into the permanence of being. What more eloquent testimonial could be adduced of the portion of eternity dwelling in the human soul?

The epigraph of this chapter is from the *Epic of Gilgamesh.* Its most recent translator in French in a scholarly edition sums up the lot of Gilgamesh in this simple phrase: "The great human being unwilling to die." Against a thousand obstacles, through forests, across mountains, over oceans, Gilgamesh journeys in quest of the plant that is to secure him immortality. Three millennia old, charged with anguish and tears, this text is truly the poem of the human being's irrepressible aspiration to immortality.[8]

Conclusion of Part 5

IN THE PAGES OF THE FIFTH PART, we have sought to explain why one and the same soul abides throughout the course of one's life. The oneness of all of the bodily, sensible, and spiritual operations is founded on a principle that remains identical, beneath the current of consciousness. This is the case with the human being, as we experience self-awareness, unity, and identity within us. And this raised consciousness bases the attribution of the totality of all personal phenomena on one and the same center, the "I."

We think, further, that these most recent chapters have explained why the human soul, as spirit, is not extinguished at the moment of death. Even here below, our intellective and volitional operations are performed without the collaboration of the body. Abstraction of ideas, invariable definitions universally applicable to the most widely varied concrete individuals, artistic creation, all testify to the presence of a power transcending time and space—these are the phenomena that moved Aristotle to write, "It is unreasonable to admit that the intellect is intermixed with the body" (*On the Soul* 3.4.429a.24). In another of his works, he gives the reason: ". . . For a bodily activity has nothing in common with the activity of the intellect" (*On the Generation of Animals* 2.3.736b.29).

We can draw the same conclusion with respect to the sphere of the free will. Since it is able to resist the pressures of the outer and inner world, freedom emancipates the human being with regard to the things of the material universe. Above all, the ultimate reason of this domination is found precisely in the object of the will: the absolute, universal, complete Good. Indeed, this good can appear in pursuits and delights altogether incompatible mutually: in repose and in work, in study or in action, in pleasures and in austerity—we could go on and on. The universal, absolute Good "presents a character of form with reference to all of the particular conditions in which it is realized, without ever allowing itself to be exhausted there."[9]

We may conclude, then, that, even though our intellective activities and our volitional activities are exercised in constant contact with acts of sensible knowing and with the tendencies of the bodily appetites, still their transcendence of the world of matter is evident. The human soul, the first substantial principle of these operations, cannot be entirely enveloped by the horizon of the material universe.

How could we not altogether subscribe to the tenet of St. Thomas Aquinas? "The human soul is a kind of horizon, and a boundary, as it were, between the corporeal world and the incorporeal world" (*Contra Gentiles* 2.68).

Part 6

Conclusion:
The Human Person

The person is what is most perfect in all of nature.
                                        —St. Thomas Aquinas

General Conclusion:
The Soul and the Person

It is a high dignity to subsist in a rational nature.
—St. Thomas Aquinas

IN THE FOREWORD at the beginning of this book, we quoted the Greek poet who celebrates the human being: "Of all the marvels of nature, the greatest is the human being." To conclude this book, we yield the floor to St. Thomas Aquinas. In his *Summa Theologiae,* with just as much enthusiasm, he writes: "The person is what is most perfect in all of nature" (I, q. 29, a. 3). It is like an echo of Sophocles' *Antigone* in this theoretical treatise. The difference between them is that St. Thomas explains where the reason of the excellence of the human being is to be found. This reason is that the human being is the only being in nature to subsist in a spiritual soul.

Over the course of our description of the work performed by the soul in order to lead the human being to the perfection of her nature, we were moving toward this conclusion. Gradually we came to understand that it is thanks to her nature of spirit that she arrives at the dignity of the person. All of her operations—corporeal, sensible, and spiritual—are accomplished by the soul in order that a human person may find birth, growth, maturation, and completion. We should be remiss in our effort to show the "why" of the existence of a spiritual soul in the human being if we failed to devote some space to an analysis of the person. The following pages, then, will serve as a comprehensive conclusion to this book.

The Human Person

THE NOTION OF THE PERSON is one of the most difficult to set forth. And yet its reality is evident, and its value is obvious to the awareness from the very start. We may begin by analyzing its external projections.

I read, for example, in the newspaper: "We noted the presence of the following personalities at the ceremony." And the names of a number of individuals of the city who are outstanding in political, military, ecclesiastical, and other affairs follow. In this case, the notion of personality designates a human being who stands out above others by reason of his functions, his offices, his merits. In this sense, we attach the word "personality" to an individual who is head and shoulders above his fellow citizens. One accedes to this dignity by separating oneself from the ordinary mass of human beings and by offering a unique type to the admiration of others. As we see, the notion of personality implies the attributes of distinction, separation, individual worth, uniqueness.

There is also such a thing as a moral personality, a moral person. In this case, "personality" denotes a more interior expression. We attribute a moral personality to someone who does not simply submit to the customs of the day and current opinions. Capable of breaking with the habits of his milieu, independent in his judgment, his is an action detached from that of the mass of humankind. In this case as well we find the characteristics, already noted, that go with this denotation: a certain manner of separation from others, of rising above them, a consistency, and a freedom.

To sum up: What constitutes a personality is expressed in a group of predicates: a propensity for emerging from a grouping, separation, distinction, independence, preeminence, consistency. These are the very attributes that we shall find, analogously, in the psychological notion of person.

The Psychological Person

From the psychological viewpoint, which is the viewpoint from which we speak of "person" in the following paragraphs, when we use that word we designate a being that has self-awareness. The person is the "I." The discovery of the "I" means becoming aware of my individual existence, separated from that of other beings. This new consciousness is experienced by some as a unique event in their life. In that case they are awakened forever to the mystery of their subjectivity. Joy or anguish accompanies this experience. Julien Green confides to us that, in his case, the discovery was a sorrowful one:

> Everyone has known that singular instant at which we feel suddenly separated from the rest of the world by the fact that we are ourself and not what surrounds us. I leave to the specialists the concern of explaining these things, in which I admit I do not have clear vision. All that I retain is that, for my part, I left a paradise at that moment. It was the melancholic hour in which the first person singular makes its entry into human life, jealously to keep front and center stage to our last breath. True, I was happy afterwards, but not as I had been before, in the Eden from which we are driven by the fiery angel called "I."[1]

Understood as self-awareness, the person is a "phenomenal" reality, a reality available to observation. My personhood is available to introspection. It has a history—a genesis, a growth, a maturity. It knows, then, the vicissitudes of all that, in our material universe, is called to develop organically, to live. We shall describe the various elements of this gradual "consciousness-raising" on the part of the "I." Since we are orienting these analyses toward a grasp of the metaphysical person, we shall remark especially, in these descriptions, the manner in which the person conquers itself by the search for interior unity at the heart of multiplicity, of necessity at the heart of contingency of situations, of fidelity to itself at the heart of change. This birthing of the "I" is an experience at once exalting and painful.

The Organic "I"

The genesis of the "I" takes place amidst our body itself. The feeling of our distinction from the world and other persons is born at the level of the body. We shall call the "I" that we shall be considering from this angle, from the viewpoint of the participation of the body, the "organic I." After having noted the obstacles presented by the body for the construction of the "I," Lavelle writes:

> But what would we be without this body, which gives our being a special situation in space and time, which keeps it within certain determinate bounds, which makes it an individual and enables it to say "I"? It is an enemy, which we ceaselessly disparage, but it is also the most tender of friends. Yes, it limits us, but in limiting us it makes of us a unique, original, and distinct being.[2]

The body, then, is part of the person. It is "my" body. It is integrated into the "I." I attribute to "myself" all that happens to it. And contrary to what Plato and spiritualist philosophy affirm, the body is not an object for the "I." It is not a tool of the "I." It is a part of the "I," to the point that, without the body, the human being is no longer a human person. There would no longer be that totality comprising, in oneness, body and soul. We realize, then, that it is through the body that the experience of the "I" begins. It is the body that makes an individual of our being, permitting it to say "I." And with that we have a new extension of our substantial unity of body and soul.

We also come to see that this is the level at which we must integrate the invaluable analyses of depth psychology when it comes to the psychological development of the child.[3] We have no intention of summarizing these studies here. Of the information they furnish us, let us retain simply the following.

From birth to the age of three, the child gradually disengages himself from the world in which he is at first totally immersed. He has lived nine months in total dependence on his mother, but now his birth has marked a breach with this first milieu of life. It is the first disengagement among a whole series of breaches whose purpose is to produce a living organism existing for itself. Weaning, for example, will be "somewhat like a new birth—the consummate breach with the maternal organism."[4]

During the first three years, the child's life is devoted to the construction of her body. It is this construction that will make her an individual—a being separated from the other bodies of the world but undivided in itself. First, as rooted in the world, she will take her distance from things by means of her body itself. By the movement of her hands and feet, by her attempts to walk, she wins her independence. "Nearing three, the child is now someone who has completed the building of his body, which has disengaged him from the surrounding milieu by means of an exploratory activity. He has used this activity to establish certain affective ties with his environment, into which he now begins consciously to insert himself."[5] We cannot say more in the framework of a succinct introduction. But we think that this will suffice for gaining the intuition that the history of our "I" has humble beginnings, and that the construction of our body represents an important step in this history.

The Psychological "I"

But the "I" finds other ground on which to move out as well– that of the psychic activities. While the constitutive bodily experience of the organic "I" supplies the child with the sensation of his bodily independence, the activities of intellect and will supply other elements, enhancing his disengagement from the world of things, along with a self-localization. Let us attempt to describe how these activities cooperate in the production of a self-awareness that, for that matter, is never completely finished.

Contribution of the intellect. It is easy to imagine that the acts of the intellect contribute to the creation of the "I." The intellect knows the very being of things. It bears on the *in se,* the in-itself, of reality. The estimative power of the animal perceives things only in terms of the circuit of its biological interest. It is an essentially subjective knowledge. The nobility of spirit resides in its capacity for attention to the being of things. The intellect is the pure mirror of things. It reflects their "act," their reality, their density, their proper value. The operation of the intellect is reception of the other *as* other.

But this objectivity of knowledge can only be realized if the thing is known in its otherness. It will be only the act of the intellect, then, that will realize perfectly the classic definition of knowledge: "Being another as other." But how might one be another without awareness of self by the very fact of being the other pole of this duality in union? This reflection on the part of the intelligence is accomplished very particularly in the judgment, an operation in which the mind consciously finds itself in confrontation with reality. St. Thomas several times asserts the thesis that the judgment implies this illuminating folding back of the mind upon itself. Here, for example, is what he writes in his *De Veritate* (On Truth).

> Truth is found in the intellect because it is produced by the intellect and known by it. It is produced by the operation of the judgment, whose term is the very reality of things. Furthermore, it is known by the intellect precisely when the latter reflects on its act. It reflects on its act because it knows it, but further, it grasps the relationship it has with the thing. This grasp can be realized only if the intellect knows the very nature of its act, that is, if it perceives the nature of the intellect as a faculty whose property it is to conform itself to the real. Thus, the intellect knows truth by reflecting upon itself. (q. 1, a. 9)

In these very acts of intelligence and freedom, there is a presence of the soul to itself, a habitual awareness of itself. For our purposes, we must now add that this habitual awareness of itself, when it passes to act by the operations of the intellect, constitutes precisely the psychological "I." The intellect's reflexive knowledge in this case is an experience. It is in intuitive certitude that the soul possesses its most individual existence.

> As it is connatural to our intellect, in the state of the present life, to turn toward material, sensible things, it occurs as a result that our intellect grasps itself as actualized by abstract similitudes of sensible things by the light of the agent intellect. The latter plays the role of actualizer with regard to intelligibles themselves, on account of which the passible intellect performs the act of intelligence. It is not by its essence, then, but by its act that our intellect knows itself. (St. Thomas Aquinas, *Summa Theologiae* I, q. 87, a. 1)

It is in an individual act, produced by me, that the intellect and consequently the soul are known by themselves. It is the individual act, produced by me, that is the mediator of this self-knowledge. Therefore what is perceived is not the essence of the soul but the soul in its individuality and concreteness. It grasps itself as the existing concrete principle of the operations emerging from it here and now.

> Indeed it is the substance of the soul—not its abstract substance, its nature, but its real, existing, concrete, living substance—that is finally experienced at the term of the observation of awareness. The soul, by itself, grasps itself by itself—not its whole self but itself nonetheless. It perceives itself directly, at the source of its intellectual acts. Thus the soul can hand down its verdict, in all of its realistic vigor: I perceive experientially that it is I who think—I, that is, the being, the concrete, real substance that I am.[6]

These observations afford us an understanding of consciousness of self as a phenomenon. They yield the formal reason for this act. We understand how this act arises at the heart of the activity of intellective knowledge as its necessary accompaniment. Its ontological root is the habitual consciousness of the soul. The soul is intelligible in itself, directly, because it is immaterial. And immateriality and intelligibility, we recall, are proportional. Furthermore, the soul is also intelligent. In its present condition, it is true, it can perform an act of self-cognition, self-awareness, only if it first knows the realities of the world. But let the intellect act on any object, and it cannot fail to have, as well, as its object that intelligible that is itself, ever present to itself. Thus, in our individual soul we always have this presence of the soul as object to the soul as subject, but in the state of *habitus,* that is, of expectation, of promise, of thrust. Intelligible and intellect embrace in the same being, constituting what is called habitual self-awareness. This habitual awareness is nothing other than the soul itself, the substance of the soul as inclination to know itself, readiness for this actual becoming conscious of itself. It is the substance of the soul, as a seed already formed, that asks only to fructify in actual awareness. It is the very being of a being that is on the point of self-awareness.

> Without the innate inclination to know itself in its substance, which is the basis of the inner structure of all spirit, and which springs from the congenital information [the act of the soul-form in bestowing identity on a substance] of its self-intelligent substance by its self-intelligible substance, the reflection of consciousness would not have its organic cause in the soul. It would constitute an ensemble of phenomena hanging in thin air, without anything to link one to another.[7]

Self-awareness! Its root, then, is to be found in the very structure of the soul—in the inclination of this structure to envelop itself as subject and object of knowing intimately joined in the same being. Its flower is the act of knowing of the soul by itself, an act suddenly emerging thanks to the mediation of the act of intelligence bearing upon an object of this world. The limitation of this act is to be able to be exercised only when accompanied first by an overt knowledge of another being. Its promise is to be the path leading to the mystery of subjectivity itself. But this path of subjectivity is discovered by the soul also in the experience of freedom.

Contribution of freedom. This experience of the psychological "I" is enhanced by the acts of free choice. Let us return to Lavelle's reflection, cited above.

> Freedom and consciousness are but one. After all, how would one be free, and deprived of awareness? And of what could one have consciousness but of the being that one gives oneself, in separating oneself from the world, but in turning toward the world an initiative proper to ourselves? The degrees of liberty and the degrees of consciousness grow proportionately.[8]

As we have seen, in the free act it is I who am the cause of the action I posit. I create the motives of this action. That is to say, the action is "mine" in a new way. The free act is an act whose source is the "I." It depends on the deliberation I have with myself. In positing such an act, the "I" cannot fail to discover itself. For Maine de Biran, as is well known, the "I" resides altogether in the awareness of free activity. It is by the effort of the will being exercised on organic resistance that the "I" is constituted. According to Maine de Biran, we ought not to say, "I think, therefore I am," but "I will, therefore I am." And he writes:

> We cannot know ourselves as individual persons without feeling ourselves to be causes relative to certain effects or movements produced in the organic body. The cause or force actually applied to move the body is an acting force called "will." The "I" is completely identical with this active force.[9]

A free act is an act that emerges from the very depths of the subject. It is an act that owes as little as possible to pressures from without and to the thrusts of our nature. The outer world and the internal data of nature are in the free act, but as matter that it models, as the resistance in which it finds its fulcrum for its exercise. But at the moment of decision, freedom gives the subject the power to snatch itself from the weight of habits, of ready-made judgments, of the world around, of what psychoanalysis calls the id and the super-ego. The free act rules over instinctual drives, the passions, heredity, the suggestions of the imagination. A free act demonstrates in the individual an interiority that conquers its determinisms.

We have said that the organic "I" especially demonstrates individuality. The individual is a being separated from other beings by its body, which has a biological life for itself alone. And yet it is inserted into a species, and the principles of its species permeate it with their dynamisms. Now, the individual attains to the dignity of the person when, by freedom, it dominates this given of nature, when it molds and shapes it, when it subjects it to its own spiritual ends. Thus, it has rightly been said, "the individual is the synthesis of nature and freedom."

Finally, the free act is an act issuing from the interpenetration of the intellect and will. These two faculties determine each other mutually, forming a practical judgment by which the subject asserts itself in confrontation with the world. Now, the acts of each of these faculties become objects for the other faculty.

> The intellect perceives the act of the will by the reflux of the movement of the will in the intellect, since the two faculties are united in the essence of the soul. The will, in a sense, moves the intellect when I understand that I will; and the intellect moves the will when I will something because I understand that it is good. (St. Thomas Aquinas, *III Sent.* d. 23, q. 1, a. 2, ad 3)

In the foregoing pages, we have seen that the actuation of the immaterial faculties is accompanied by an enlightening folding back of the faculty upon itself, immediately entailing a folding of this faculty over the individual substance of the soul.

If in every speculative judgment the subject knows itself in asserting truth, this awareness is even more accentuated in a practical judgment. In the speculative judgment, the subject is measured by the object that imposes upon it its "evidence," its quality of being evident. In the practical judgment, the subject takes its distance, if we may so say, from the object. The subject has control over its judgment. The final judgment—the one that will determine the free act—is governed by the subject by reason of its basic project, in which it defines itself in its individual essence, or its person. The free judgment is truly the expression of subjectivity. In it the "I" recognizes itself in its consistency. From the voluntary act flows an exceptional sensation of our individual existence.

This sense of existence is so strong that a whole philosophical current identifies existence and freedom. For existentialism, only the human being exists, because only the human being, among the beings of this world, is free. By her freedom, the person is promoted to the dignity of *causa sui,* "cause of herself." And only that which is cause of itself "exists" in the proper sense of the word.

Consciousness and existence. For existentialism, the existence of consciousness is reducible to consciousness of one's existence. The entire being of the human being is reducible to the act of awareness. And this act is realized in the acts of knowing and of freedom. And of course, in going out of itself to meet another being—which is the act of intentionality of knowing—the subject appears, and hence becomes a being-for-itself. The same thing occurs, analogously, with freedom. In projecting himself toward the future, toward his "possibles," the human being exists. This is what Sartre means when he writes: "All conscious existence exists as consciousness of existing."[10]

For Sartre, then, the psychological "I," the appearance of self to self, is the person's whole being. He writes:

Consciousness has nothing of the substantial about it. It is pure "appearance," in the sense that it exists only to the extent that it appears. But it is precisely because it is pure appearance, because it is a total void (since the entire world is outside of it), it is because of this identity in it of appearance and existence, that it can be regarded as the absolute.[11]

As we see, the human subject is reduced to the "I," to the act of self-awareness. And as that subject appears to itself by means of its freedom and its knowing, whose cause it is, it exists by itself. It is an absolute. For this reason Sartre rejects substance as a basis of the phenomenon of awareness. Consciousness is based on itself.

But it is too early to stop there, en route, and arbitrarily renounce any transcendence of the phenomenon. It has been said, and most justly:

True, the bond between freedom and existence is evident, and its assertion a commonplace in contemporary philosophy. However, this philosophy tends to reduce human existence. The link tightens to the point of identity, and metaphysics is eclipsed by a phenomenology of the "I." Now, not even the subtlest phenomenology can replace metaphysics. Beyond descriptions, reductions, and analyses, the mind, invincibly, seeks to understand, and there is no authentic understanding that will not be founded on being.[12]

And so we must also speak of the metaphysical aspect of the person. Philosophical psychology opens out onto ontology.

Metaphysical Root of the Person

We must take our leave of the domain of acting, in which the human subject exercises self-awareness and possesses himself in a unique fashion among the existents of the world. We must delve even more deeply into the interiority of the subject, to discover there the metaphysical root of the person. There is indeed a psychological person in the human being, and this has been the subject of our considerations up until now. But the human being also contains a metaphysical person. Not that there are two persons here, two beings. It is one and the same person who, hidden at first on the level of being, appears to himself on the level of acting. The "I" could never come to flower in the act of consciousness unless it had as its root, in its very being, subsistence.

But how are we to render this mysterious reality evident? We shall offer two reflections of a metaphysical order.

First, the psychological person formally consists in a conscious appropriation, by a subject, of her actions. The conscious subject perceives that her actions are hers. To appropriate one's actions and to know it are to possess oneself twice. Now, this belonging-to-self, realized on the level of action, is only the projection of a more basic belonging-to-self in the line of existence. Philosophically speaking, action is situated in the prolongation of existence. It is the tension of a being that would "exist more," more authentically. Such is the metaphysical perspective of the free act, as we have seen. From this angle, intellective knowing appears as an attempt to emerge from the confines in which our species imprisons us, in order to become, to "exist"—the act of all beings. But in order to be able thus to belong to ourselves in the order of action, we must first belong to ourselves in the order of existence. Therefore we shall define the metaphysical person by calling it that which gives a spiritual nature to appropriate to itself existence, to possess existence for itself. Or better, the person gives a being to exercise existence, the most fundamental act of being.

Second, there is a multitude of existents in the world. This rose, this dog, this person, exercise an existence of their own. We could imagine that these things are but parts of a whole, threads in the fabric of the universe. Nothing could be further from the truth. What astonishes the metaphysician is precisely that these things have an existence all their own. This rose has an existence that belongs to it as much as does its bright color. This bird has an existence as much its own as its song. The rose and the bird have appropriated existence. Existence is their primordial good, which they possess in independence. And the person is that which gives to a human subject to have an incommunicable existence. This radical independence in being explains the fact that she will be able to perform her own actions. And if it is easier to understand this appropriation on the level of acting, this is because we do not really realize that the adjective "being" signifies one thing: that a being (the noun) performs the act of acts, existence.

In calling existence an act, we do not mean that it is an ac*tion*. Let us note the following judicious observations.

Since to exist is an act, and since the notion of act is formed by analogy with action, when speaking of *esse* ["to be," the act of existing] it is difficult to avoid the vocabulary of action entirely. Let us say, then, once and for all, that, in employing these formulae we have no intention of making an activity of being. We intend only, first, to emphasize the analogy between existing and acting, both of these being not only acts, but "second acts," ultimate acts, acts whose concept excludes all potentiality; and second, to emphasize the radication, the rooting, of acting in being. And when we say that a being exercises the act of existing, we intend simply to assert the "in itself" of the being—that ontological depth that makes it something else than a phenomenon or an idea. True, "to be" is not an action; but it is the presupposition of every action.[13]

Let us yield to our astonishment that so many and such varied things in the world should perform the act of existence. To exercise existence is to perform the most important act, the one that decides all of the others. Indeed, without it the others could not emerge. This bird that I watch describing unpredictable figures in the sky performs the act of existence before all else. And that is extraordinary! The exercise of existence contains, as it were, an original self-assertion—an *obstinacy*-to-be, if we may thus express ourselves—that future actions only realize the more, if according to their plan.

Now, the foundation of this tendency to exist for oneself, to exercise the act of existence in appropriation, to render this existence strictly incommunicable, is what we call subsistence. It is subsistence that constitutes, in subjects of existence, the specific natures of the world. (These subjects are called "supposits," if they are other than human, and "persons" if they are human.)

Subsistence is a concrete principle in the very being of a person. It is a "perfection," a concrete attribute, of an ontological order, since it has an immediate relationship to existence. It is not existence. Existence in itself is "communicable" (it can be found in more than one individual)—that is, in its pure line of existence. Nor may subsistence be confused with essence. Essence, too, is communicable, since it is multiplied in the individuals of a species. True, essence is ordered to existence, but not as that which appropriates existence—not as that which brings it about that the essence of human being belong to Peter, for example. It might appear more likely that the appropriation of existence should flow from individuation. Is not individuation that which brings it about that a being of this world is separate from every other by reason of the matter that it possesses? Could this separation not have as one of its effects that Peter receive existence for himself? Still, it will be enough to reflect on the fact that individuality is an effect of matter. What individualizes a body in the world is the first accident, or incidental, that flows from matter: quantity. But matter and quantity are concrete passive "principles." And what is passive in itself cannot be in itself what exercises the act of existing. To exercise that force by which a thing maintains itself above nothingness and outside of its causes, cannot be the deed of a purely passive principle. Thus, we must posit an entity that is really distinct from existence, essence, and individuation all at once. It will be a perfection sui generis: subsistence cannot be reduced to any or all of the members of the trio just cited. It is mysterious, in that it constitutes a human nature a subject of existence, a person. We may not consider it a reality separated, divided, from essence and existence, as if wafting above these two principles and using them as instruments. Subsistence is part of the concrete being. It is by subsistence that the individual essence of a human being will be able to exercise for itself the very act of existing.

In the case of the human person, subsistence must have a "perfection," or concrete attribute, a value, of the same order as the spiritual nature whose incommunicability it is its assignment to secure.

St. Thomas extols the value of the person in these terms: "The person is what is most perfect in all of nature–that which subsists in a rational nature" (*Summa Theologiae* I, q. 29, a. 3).

Ordinarily so reserved in his style, when he speaks of the person he lavishes the superlatives. "It is a high dignity to subsist in a rational nature," he writes again (ibid., ad 2). Have the partisans of a "Christian personalism" that implies disdain for St. Thomas mediated such texts?

But if this is the highest perfection, then we shall have to say that what exists are not natures or essences but supposits, persons. Now we understand that essence and existence are but for the person, in order that a person maintain itself in being, outside of its causes, and that it expand in acting. The person, then, is the end, the purpose, of all that it possesses. All that is given to it is given only that it "be" still more, on the level of its actions. Granted, it is of sovereign importance to a person that he take cognizance, be conscious, of himself, that he act freely, that he give himself in love. It is for such "self-perfection" that he has received a spiritual, and indeed a bodily, nature. But long before a person is "perfected" in the order of acting, he surpasses in value all that exists in nature. We are fond of these reflections of Stefanini:

> I am preceded by myself. There is an in-itself of my being that the for-itself will never equal. What I am in the intimacy of my being overflows my act all the more triumphantly as the latter cleaves more tenaciously to a constructive effort of inner up-building. Self-creation is a magnificent human ambition, and G. Gentile has developed it in the form of a dream. [But] let us open our eyes. We observe that, far as our act may extend, we never arrive at nourishing our own roots.[14]

The value of the person consists in the fact that her nature and existence belong to her as her own. Subsistence stamps the seal of possession on this being. It inscribes, in the nature it crowns and in the existence it acquires for itself, in the very being it makes its own, a tendency to realize itself further, for itself, on the plane of acting. The subsistence of the person conceives itself only if its being really belongs to it.

To the question, What is your person? I cannot answer, . . .

". . . It is my body, my soul, my intellect, my will, my freedom, my mind." None of these things, ultimately, is person. They are all, so to speak, the matter of person. Person itself is the fact that all of this exists under the category of belonging-to-self. On the other hand, this "matter" does really exist under this category, and thus is found entirely marked by its sign. The complete reality of the human being, and not only his or her consciousness or freedom, for example, belongs to the domain of the person–is taken in charge by it and is found determined by its dignity.[15]

On the basis of these reflections on the metaphysical person, we can deduce three tendencies inscribed in the very structure of the person.

Encounter of Persons: Dialogue

The human person is, first of all, open to other persons. "The primitive experience of person is the experience of the second person. The 'you,' and in it the 'we,' precedes the 'I,' or at least accompanies it."[16]

It is a fact that the infant perceives another well before knowing himself. Doubtless the recognition of other persons before our own and our dependence with regard to them are the marks of our finitude. It is becoming more and more acknowledged that the success of the person is tied to the quality of the infant's exchanges with the family community, first, and then with society at large. Max Scheler makes a powerful observation: "The human being lives first of all, and principally, in others, and not in himself. He lives more in the community than in his own individual."[17]

Thus, dialogue attaches directly to the person. It is an elemental tendency of the person to enter into relationships with others. Of course, every being tends to communicate its "perfections," its concrete attributes. Once a being is "in act," once it exists, under one angle, it is constituted an "efficient cause," a driving cause. Every being influences another. The bird rejoices nature with its song. The rose overwhelms us with its glow. As for us, we ourselves experience this spontaneous need to give. But in the "I," there is a new quality of communication: dialogue. In dialogue, persons meet, even when it bears on purely objective matters. In the voice, the look, the gesture, the smile or serious mien, there are always signs that reveal the "I." A purely material being communicates its qualities. As for the person, it can give *itself.* A purely material being undergoes external influences. As for the person, it is able to receive another person. Gift and receipt: such are the modalities according to which the interpersonal exchange takes place.

And is it not rather significant that we never think but in an internal language? Then it is the least step to utterance, to external language. External language is a spiritual space in which two persons exchange their ideas, their feelings. Dialogue, then, is essential to the birth and growth of the "I." "Person, under the form of dialogue, is essentially ordered to the other person. It is by nature destined to become the 'I' of a 'You.' The person who would be elementally unique does not exist."[18] It is interesting to note on this point that Christianity teaches that God is Word, in three Persons, and that the fundamental divine mystery is an eternal exchange, among those Persons, of knowing and love.

At the same time, dialogue is conceivable only between persons. For dialogue, I must first recognize in the other person an independent subject of existence, an interiority, a capacity for response, a freedom—in a word, a subjectivity. But such an attitude supposes a knowledge of the other that will be steeped in affectivity.

Discovery of the Value of the Person: Love

Dialogue is one of the forms of union that are appropriate for persons who love one another. "Aristophanes said that those who love each other would like to become, from the two that they are, only one. But because this would then be the disappearance of the two, or of one of the two, they seek the only union that will suit: that of life in common, conversation, and other, similar, things" (St. Thomas Aquinas, *Summa Theologiae* I-II, q. 28, a. 1, ad 2).

Now, if dialogue supposes recognition of the other, love does the same, and even more so. It consents to the existence of the other—even stimulates it in a certain sense. It is the quality of love to promote the individual existence of the beloved. The beloved is not in the lover as a double, a pure representation, a detached form of his real existence. But he is there according to his whole self. He is there in the lover as that which attracts him, inclines toward him, as that which makes him come out of himself. Love is ecstatic (Greek *ek*, "out of," *stat-*, "stand"). It is ravished by the unique value of the person it discovers.

It is to Scheler's credit to have so forcefully phrased the primacy of love in the knowledge of the person.

> The individual person is given to us only in the act of love, and his value, as an individual value, is revealed to us only in the course of this act. Nothing could be more mistaken than the "rationalism" that seeks to justify love for an individual person by his particularities, his acts, his works, his manner of being and behaving.[19]

We can surely do a philosophy of the person. After all, the person has structures, which can be the object of a theory. The pages immediately preceding show this. But when we say that it is love that enables us to know the person, we are speaking of the "individual" person. The person of my friend Peter, for example, is not knowable by pure intellect. The intellect shields, objectifies reality. Now, the individual subject cannot be "objectified." The "I" of another—and the same is true for mine—is impenetrable to the intellect alone. Maritain writes on this subject:

> Subjectivity as subjectivity is non-conceptualizable. It is an unknowable chasm—unknowable by way of notion, concept or representation, by way of any science whatever, introspection, psychology or philosophy. How could it be otherwise, since any reality known by concept, notion, or representation is known as object, and not as subject? Subjectivity as such, by definition, escapes what we know of ourselves notionally.[20]

But when we say that the individual person is known by love, we must append a most important observation. In itself, love does not know. But it brings the intellect a new penetration and gives it to know what, alone, it cannot know. In Thomism, we call this knowledge "knowledge by connaturality." This means, for the case before us, that the love of friendship gives us to be able to make judgments in areas that otherwise escape the investigation of theoretical knowledge. What could never be an "object" for it—the individual subject—the intellect, which love envelops and elevates, can penetrate, and very intimately.

It is here that we appreciate all of the import of affectivity. Thanks to affectivity, and by it alone, we are able to enter into the universe of persons and discover their inestimable value. "The person is the substance to which all acts attach that are performed by a human being. Inaccessible to theoretical knowledge, it is revealed to us only by the individual intuition."[21] It is love that enables a mother to know her son in a unique manner. Without this knowledge of the heart, no one would do justice to our being.

The Person's Aspiration to Immortality

Finally, the human person grasps itself as possessing a value superior to the sum of all material values. And this not only because, as Pascal said, "when the universe topples, the human being will still be more noble than what kills him, because he knows that he dies, and the universe knows nothing of the advantage it has over him" (*Pensées,* Brunschwig, p. 347). But this is true in yet another sense, because "when the universe topples, the human being knows obscurely that he cannot die."[22]

If I give away my material goods, I have the certitude that I am worth more than they. If I give my life, or if I risk it, as so many persons do all over the world every day, I am sure that I cannot die.

> At this point we face a paradox. On the one hand, nothing in the world is more precious than a singular human person. On the other hand, nothing in the world is more extravagant, more exposed to all sorts of dangers, than the human being. And this is as it must be. What is the meaning of this paradox? It is perfectly clear. We have here a sign that the human being knows very well that death is not an end, but a beginning. He knows very well, in the secret depths of his own being, that he can run all risks, squander his life, and dissipate his goods here below, because he is immortal.[23]

This knowledge, by the person herself, of her immortality is a knowledge in the form of instinct—a knowledge not founded on reasonings, not mentally argued but nevertheless implied in these deeds of generosity, of forgetfulness of self, comported by the fact of risking death. It is a knowledge not produced for itself but immersed in acts. Here there are no judgments in the strict sense, nor developed concepts. It is a dark, underground knowledge.

Meanwhile, it is possible to find the reason for this certitude. It comes from the fact that the "I" grasps itself as the invariable, constant center of transitory phenomena and states of awareness. The "I" grasps itself now as independent of time, and therefore immortal. After all, death is situated in time.

But this is also why death is incomprehensible and unacceptable. It is a scandal for the mind, a piece of "non-sense." This sensation of the absurd represents the person's typical reaction in the face of death. The person is a whole, integrating soul and body. But being spiritual as soul, it cannot understand why the body is not always united to the soul.

In the human being, then, there is an aspiration to the immortality of the whole, that is, of her mind and her body. But how could this be, since, in fact, the human being dies. Would it be possible that this aspiration could be fulfilled?

> Yes, given the omnipotence of God, there is no impossibility of a sort of reincorporation of the soul in flesh and blood, a sort of restoration of the human integrity. But human reason can only conceive this possibility. It cannot go further, and that is why, in the matter of the supreme aspiration of the human person for immortality, the immortality of the human being, human reason halts, remains silent and in reverie.[24]

Notes

Part 1
The Human Being's Sensory Life

1. Paul Claudel, *La cantate à trois voix* (Pléiade, 1957), 329.
2. Jacques Maritain, *Réflexions sur l'intelligence et sa vie propre* (Desclée de Brouwer, 1930), 106.
3. Paul Claudel, *La sensation du divin*, Etudes carmélitaines, Nos sens et Dieu (Desclée, 1954), 20.
4. Maritain, *Réflexions sur l'intelligence*, 106.
5. P. Chauchard, *Le cerveau et le conscience* (Seuil, 1960), 104.
6. Paul Claudel, *Cinq grandes odes* (Pléiade, 1957), 241.

Part 2
Human Beings: Their Intellectual Life

1. Martin Heidegger, *Questions II* (Gallimard, 1968), 215.
2. Anne Perrier, *Les noms de l'arbre* (Empreintes, 1989), 15.
3. Rainer Maria Rilke, *Oeuvres*, vol. 2, *Poésie* (Seuil, 1972), 508.
4. Jacques Maritain, *L'intuition créatrice dans l'art et la poésie* (Desclée de Brouwer, 1966), 91.
5. Jacques Maritain, *Réflexions sur l'intelligence et sa vie propre* (Desclée de Brouwer, 1930), 106.
6. Jean-Paul Sartre, *La Nausée* (Gallimard, 1938), 179.
7. *Approches sans entraves* (Fayard, 1973), 271.
8. Jacques Maritain, *Les sept leçons sur l'être* (Téqui), 97.

9. Jacques Maritain, *Court traité de l'existence et de l'existant* (Hartmann, 1947), 41.

10. Paul Claudel, *Nos sens et Dieu,* Etudes carmélitaines (Desclée, 1954), 11.

11. J. Dombrovski, *Le singe qui vient réclamer son crâne* (Verdieu, 1991), 146.

12. J. Joubert, *Pensées* (Paris: Didier, 1883), 2:50.

13. Paul Claudel, *Cinq grandes odes* (Pléiade, 1957), "Quatrième Ode," p. 267.

Part 3
Human Beings: Their Affective Life

1. Montaigne, *Précis de Psychologie* (Paris: Rivière, 1946), 499.

2. Anne Perrier, *Les noms de l'arbre* (Empreintes, 1989), 11.

3. Ibid., 49.

4. Rainer Maria Rilke, *Oeuvres,* vol. 2, *Poésie* (Seuil, 1972), 386.

5. Jacques Maritain, *Sept leçons sur l'être* (Téqui, 1933), 78.

6. In O. F. Bollnow, *Les tonalités affectives* (Neuchâtel: Baconnière, 1953), 30.

7. Ibid., 35.

8. Maritain, *Sept leçons,* 58–60.

9. Eupalinos, *L'âme et la danse* (Gallimard, 1944), 146.

10. J. Joubert, *Pensées* (Paris: Didier, 1883), 2:261.

Part 4
Human Beings: Their Freedom and Subjectivity

1. Yves Simon, *Traité du Libre-Arbitre* (Liège, 1951), 108.

2. Ibid.

3. Louis Lavelle, *Les Puissances du Moi* (Flammarion, 1948), 139–40.

4. Friedrich Nietzsche, *Ainsi parlait Zarathoustra* (Robert Laffont), 291–95.

5. Fyodor Dostoyevsky, *Les Démons* (Pléiade), 649.

6. Jacques Maritain, *Neuf leçons sur la philosophie morale* (Téqui), 49.

Part 5
Human Beings: Soul and Spirit

1. Jean-Paul Sartre, *L'Etre et le Néant* (Gallimard, N.R.F.), 13.
2. Ibid., 11.
3. Ibid., 12.
4. Jacques Maritain, *La philosophie bergsonienne* (Téqui, 1948), 249.
5. St. Edith Stein, *La science de la Croix* (Nauwelaerts, 1957), 170.
6. Cardinal Charles Journet, *Entretiens sur le Mystère Chrétien*, cahier 1, 85.
7. *Psychologie de l'Art*, vol. 1, *Le surnaturel;* vol. 2, *L'Irréel;* vol. 3, *L'Intemporel* (Gallimard, N.R.F., 1950).
8. *L'épopée de Gilgemes*, trans. Jean Bottéro (Gallimard, N.R.F., 1992).
9. Yves Simon, *Traité du Libre Arbitre* (Liège, 1951), 46.

Part 6
Conclusion: The Human Person

1. Julien Green, *Partir avant le jour* (Grasset, 1963), 23.
2. Louis Lavelle, *Les Puissances du Moi* (Flammarion, 1948), 79.
3. J.-P. Deconchy, *Le développement psychologique de l'Enfant et de l'Adolescent* (Ouvrières, 1966).
4. Ibid., 57.
5. Ibid., 71.
6. A. Gardeil, O.P., *La Structure de l'Ame et l'Expérience mystique* (Gabalda, 1927), 2:120.
7. Ibid., 111.
8. Lavelle, *Puissances du Moi*, 140–41.
9. Maine de Biran, *Oeuvres choisies de Maine de Biran* (Aubier, 1942), 87.
10. Jean-Paul Sartre, *L'Etre et le Néant* (Gallimard, N.R.F., 1943), 20.
11. Ibid., 23.
12. J. de Finance, *Existence et Liberté* (Vitte, 1955), 30.
13. Ibid., 52n.
14. Stefanini, *Itinéraires métaphysiques* (Aubier, 1952), 113.
15. Romano Guardini, *Le Monde et la Personne* (Seuil, 1959), 139.

16. Emmanuel Mounier, "Que sais-je?" in *Le Personnalisme* (1965), 38.
17. Max Scheler, *Nature et Formes de la Sympathie* (Payot, 1928), 360.
18. Guardini, *Monde et le Personne,* 155.
19. Scheler, *Nature et Formes,* 248.
20. Jacques Maritain, *Court traité de l'existence et de l'existant* (Hartmann, 1947), 115.
21. Scheler, *Monde et le Personne,* 249.
22. I here summarize Maritain's "L'immortalité de l'homme," in *Sort de l'Homme* (Neuchâtel: Baconnière, 1943), 9–34.
23. Ibid., 12–13.
24. Ibid., 25–26.

OF RELATED INTEREST

THE DEEPEST FRESHNESS DEEP DOWN THINGS

An Introduction to the Philosophy of Being

PIERRE-MARIE EMONET

A truly accessible introduction to the fundamentals of classical philosophy and metaphysics.

In this first volume, Emonet introduces the basic principles of classic Thomistic metaphysics using clear, simple language, exploring the mystery of the origin of things in the world, their purpose, and their final end.

0-8245-1794-6; $17.95 paperback

At your bookstore or, to order directly from the publisher, please send check or money order (including $3.00 for the first book plus $1.00 for each additional book) to:

THE CROSSROAD PUBLISHING COMPANY
370 LEXINGTON AVENUE, NEW YORK, NY 10017

We hope you enjoyed The Greatest Marvel of Nature. *Thank you for reading it.*

herder & herder